The Girl Who Flaps Her Hands

Meghali Mazumdar

Published by Meghali Mazumdar, 2023.

THE GIRL WHO FLAPS HER HANDS

First edition. February 24, 2023.

ISBN: 979-8215818848

Written by Meghali Mazumdar.

Table of Contents

To Ishanvi and Bivan, who changed my world.

To caregivers around the world who devote their time to special needs kids and prepare them for this world.

"*Motherhood is about raising and celebrating the child you have, not the child you thought you would have. It's about understanding that he is exactly the person he is supposed to be. And that, if you're lucky, he just might be the teacher who turns you into the person you are supposed to be.*"

— Joan Ryan, from *The Water Giver: The Story of a Mother, a Son,* [1] *and Their Second Chance* [2]

---

1. https://www.goodreads.com/work/quotes/6732176

2. https://www.goodreads.com/work/quotes/6732176

We all have experiences and feelings we're comfortable sharing. As a writer and storyteller, I find inspiration in my own life, and when I thread the words one after the other to form a story, they flow naturally. So, most of the stories I tell are true, honest tales seen through my eyes and narrated from my perspective.

I grew up in a middle-income household in the small town of Guwahati, Assam, India, the youngest child and only daughter of Kalpana and Prafulla, who were very protective of me. For most of my childhood, I was shielded from the bigger worries of the world and grew up mingling only within my community. But I have come to realize that this sort of shielding doesn't protect a child from emotions. Like most of my friends, I had enlightening interactions and heart-breaking confrontations. In short, I lived.

By telling my story, I hope my readers will experience their own feelings. My aim is not only to come out of those experiences knowing myself a little better, but to give my readers the same chance. Often, we're too busy to feel our emotions wholly. I hope to change that.

I understand I am being vulnerable when I share my deepest emotions through my writing, but I believe these emotions make us human.

As Danish poet K. Tolnoe wrote, "Every emotion has a story to tell."

This is mine.

It's about how I became the mother I was supposed to be for my daughter, Ishanvi. So much is said about motherhood in general, the expectations versus the reality. It's a tough transition for a woman, but it can be a rewarding one.

For me, it has been life altering. Caring for my kids and watching them grow has been a privilege that came with challenges. Sometimes, the intensity of those challenges nearly dampened my spirits. But isn't that what life is about?

So, I buckle up and carry on. For the sake of my kids.

Motherhood is tough. Parenting coach Sue Atkins wrote, "There is no such thing as a perfect parent. So just be a real one."

Like billions of mothers all over the world, I'm trying.

PART 1
Before

Chapter 1: Love

The summer of 2019 was a special one for my family. I was living with the love of my life in supposedly the greatest nation in the world. I was happy because my family was finally together under one roof. At the time, there were only three of us, but it was becoming tough for us to be together in the same country. Life, however unfair, happened regardless of how we felt about it.

All that was about to change as the new year descended on us.

First, a little background:

I grew up in a small town in North-East India, an often-neglected part of my big, beautiful country. Even communication with the rest of India was challenging, so visiting America was a distant, almost unachievable dream. An astrologer who read my palm told me I would end up in America one day. I almost laughed. He didn't specify if I would be visiting or living there indefinitely, and I wasn't interested in asking.

Guwahati is a quaint and beautiful small town in the state of Assam. Whenever I picture it, I imagine lush green hills on the banks of the mighty Brahmaputra River. It rained incessantly, but I loved it. Our tea gardens are famous all over the world. Our forests are home to endangered animals and birds, most notably the one-horned rhinoceros. It was my town, but I didn't want to stay there forever, so I chose a college in Southern India, almost 2000 miles away.

After living in Guwahati for seventeen years, it was time to explore another world. Little did I know that my adventure would imperil my heart. I was so homesick I begged my parents to bring me back. I'd never been away for more than a week and didn't realize it would be so painful. How could I have known? I was terribly sad for the first six months, but I survived. I now know why. I was there to meet the love of my life.

I met Pravin accidentally. I'd built a reputation as the nice girl at the college, albeit unknowingly. I was cordial with everyone, as I'd been taught since I was a kid, always carrying a smile on my face. I didn't realize that the smile and courtesies meant so much more to the boys.

In India's engineering colleges, boys usually outnumbered girls, and I was one of the few girls without an attitude. Those aspiring engineers might someday change the world, but they were, in fact, teenagers with overactive hormones looking for companions. Because of the unbalanced sex ratio, several boys were often interested in one girl. It wasn't fair, but then, has life ever been fair?

Take beauty as an example. I have average looks for an Indian girl. "How do I know that?"

Time and again, people in my life have reminded me that I have a dusky complexion (thanks, Dad), a weird bent nose (thanks, sinusitis), and rough skin on my elbows (looking at you again, Dad). When I saw myself in the mirror, I often wondered why I looked the way I did. My father is dark-skinned, but my mother is not. I inherited his complexion, and unfortunately for me, my brothers inherited my mother's features. As they say in my country, my mother is "fair and lovely."

In India, it's much harder to be a dark-skinned girl than a dark-skinned boy. And when you're told repeatedly that your looks are less than average, you start doubting yourself. You begin to think you're not pretty enough for romantic love and are not worthy of it. Life in engineering school was so unfair that by the second semester, I'd already found a boyfriend. But the relationship wasn't going well. That's when Pravin entered my life.

It wasn't love at first sight. At least not for me. I don't believe it has to be for love to last, and it was love, after all. When I decided to date him, my world turned upside down. Nice girls didn't have two boyfriends in one semester, and Pravin was notorious for the flings he'd had before college. In India, it's an unspoken rule that you have to marry within your own community, and Pravin wasn't from my part of the country. As I was falling in love with him, I was mercilessly stripped of my "nice girl" title. I was just living my life. I didn't know that there were rules for girls.

It didn't help that Pravin was unbelievably handsome. He has since lost his charm a bit, but that's not important. He kept spoiling me with expensive gifts (by college standards), which made matters worse. We were officially the "couple no one could stand," but we were oblivious. When we were together, we created our own world and were so involved nothing else mattered. Together, we survived tornadoes of hatred and mountains of ignorance.

But that ignorance did eventually affect me. In my second year at college, I began my journey with depression, but Pravin made sure I survived, even when, at the depth of it, I became suicidal. He lived at the other end of the college campus, so I don't know how the hell he managed it. I'm indebted to him for that support and love. I had friends living in the same building who didn't care anymore. I used to beg him to let go of me, to just let me go. I'd pack my bags, but somehow, he always knew. He held my hand and heart firmly but delicately every time I tried to leave.

Within a year, I came out of my depression, believing that we were truly, madly, deeply in love. That was in the early 2000s.

Twenty years later, we share the same passion.

We graduated college with decent jobs in hand and started our work lives in different cities. Within a month, we realized we couldn't live without seeing each other every day. Eventually, Pravin chose to move to New Delhi, although it didn't hold much promise for his career. His excuse was that it didn't matter so long as he was with me. He knew how to show his love. It was unfair how much he was willing to sacrifice to be with me. Slowly, my feeling of being unworthy of love disappeared.

Almost four years after I graduated, my parents began talking about marriage, and I panicked. As pressure from both our families mounted, we decided it was time to get married. It seemed like an obvious decision, but it was not easy.

I was painfully aware that my family would never agree. Sometimes, I wonder if that was my fault, if I was too panic-stricken to give them a chance to resist.

That remains one of the biggest disappointments of my life. My family deserved better, and I should have tried harder. I was naive. I wish someone had told me to be more patient, to at least try to convince them. Pravin tried to talk sense into me, but I discounted him because he didn't know my parents. I didn't want to risk it all. I couldn't bear the thought of being forced to marry someone else.

When we finally married in December 2012, my family wasn't invited to the wedding. That gesture brought a huge storm to our lives. My parents were devastated. I'm their only daughter. They must have dreamt of giving me away with pride in their hearts and tears in their eyes. Instead, they heard the news over the phone. I couldn't even imagine what they must have felt. So I refused to think about it until years later.

When I finally thought about it, I imagined they felt pain, probably shame, but I didn't care. I'd suffered throughout my relationship with Pravin. He'd been there to support me when I needed him. I chose him without wanting to explain why. I was tired of explaining his relevance in my life. He's the most important person to me. Period.

Sometimes, we must be willing to take tough decisions, even when they might bring a lot of unhappiness to someone important. I had made my decision. But we survived, as we always do.

My parents eventually came to terms with our marriage. We took a breather and hoped our time of struggle and hardship had come to an end. We had no idea that another struggle was waiting for us a few years down the line with the birth of our daughter in 2016.

Chapter 2: A Happy Ending?

I picture all the good memories from each year and file them in my head.

2005, the year I met Pravin. 2008, the year I started my first job. 2012, the year we were married. 2016, the year our daughter was born.

In this way, I associate each year with one big positive event (or a few) and avoid remembering a bunch of terrible things. Think and remember happy times! My motto in life.

After our marriage, things changed. Pravin had to move to the United States for work. We took it positively—better pay, vacations in the US. I'd travel back and forth to visit him. Everything would be under control. And for three years, it was, until our daughter was born. We named her "Ishanvi" after the Hindu goddess of power.

Her birth brought a new set of questions. How long could we continue to live like this with a baby in our lives? For years, we'd been the leading characters in a turbulent love story. I wanted to believe we'd been blessed with a happy ending, but I wondered what a happy ending was. Did it mean the boy and girl live happily ever after? Our life together was defined by struggle—for acceptance, for validity, for survival. In the early stages of our relationship, we'd failed to gain acceptance from everyone who mattered. I'd fallen into a depression I barely survived. We nearly failed to collect our diplomas. We survived a year of constant struggle, only to realize that we were seeking acceptance from the wrong people. We were still teenagers. When we got married, my parents weren't there to give us their blessings. Then Pravin was assigned to a job in the US. Now we lived on separate continents.

How was that a happy ending?

I was away from Pravin for most of my pregnancy because his visa restrictions prevented him from traveling to India. I needed him by my side to witness that monumental moment, so I flew to America during my last trimester. I wanted him by my side when I gave birth. I would have flown to Timbuktu if need be. I believe we've been together for so long because we always choose each other, no matter what.

We still worked on different continents. I was willing to give up everything to be with him—even my financial independence. But Pravin wouldn't let me.

For the first year of her life, our daughter was with us both in Davenport, Iowa. Then my job called me back. I didn't have any more time off. Maternity leave seemed like the only option. We wanted to have another baby, so it became an acceptable option. In order to apply for another maternity leave, I'd have to have another baby. Around Ishanvi's first birthday, like a stroke of luck, I discovered I was pregnant again.

We thought it was God's way of keeping us together, but He had other plans. During lunch one day, I felt a strange pain in my stomach and immediately texted Pravin. He had gone to work. I didn't drive, so he had to take me to the doctor to check if everything was okay. It was not. I suffered a miscarriage in the eighth week of my pregnancy. I was heartbroken.

I asked the doctors if I'd miscarried from holding Ishanvi on my lap. She was a very healthy baby and loved to cuddle with me, sometimes jumping on my lap. The doctors said that was not the reason. Miscarriages are more common than we think and can happen for a variety of reasons. I realized that no one had ever talked to me about miscarriages. ***If it's so common, why weren't we talking about it?***

I wanted to talk to somebody about my grief. But I had no one. Pravin didn't carry the baby, so he didn't qualify. It was just me and my thoughts.

2017, the year I lost my baby!

That loss spiraled into a streak of grief-driven decisions. The apartment in Iowa reminded me of the baby I'd lost. Using the bathroom reminded me of the blood I'd seen. I was due at work in India soon. So, I decided it was time for a change of place.

I didn't realize how much my decision would affect Ishanvi. It was difficult for her to be away from her dad for months. It was difficult for me to see her suffer. And I had my own pain. I struggled with wanting to be a good mother and do the right thing. I should have known there is no right thing. We're all just mothers, bound to be judged and criticized by the world, and often by ourselves.

For ten days after we got back to India, Ishanvi cried looking for her dad every evening. Pravin has always been an involved father and her missing him proved it. Her screams affected me so much, I began to panic as the sun set. I had no help whatsoever. I didn't know if I could continue. I begged her to stop, but she didn't listen. I couldn't go back to Iowa where I'd lost my baby, and I couldn't explain that to her. On the eleventh day, I called my parents and told them I would go back to the US if they didn't come immediately. They rushed to New Delhi. It wasn't a nice move, but it was the only move I could think of. After they arrived, Ishanvi stopped screaming. She had someone to interact with other than me. At that point in time, we both needed a break from each other. But her screams still sometimes haunt me. I've stored them in the "unhappy memories" folder, and I don't ever want to open it.

This was our path to settling down in India, but it was hard without Pravin. We both missed him. A lot. The screaming stopped, but the heart still ached.

2018, the year Pravin and I spent the most time apart.

The separation put a lot of stress on our relationship, and for the first time in a decade, we were losing each other. I had to do something. I couldn't lose Pravin.

In the summer of 2018, we visited him for a month to celebrate Ishanvi's second birthday and to protect her from the summer heat of India. When I saw Pravin at the airport and watched Ishanvi hold on to him like a baby monkey, I realized we belonged together. I decided that no matter what was at stake, I'd spend the rest of my days with Pravin.

I saw how shattered he was at the thought that we'd leave again. More than that, it hurt me to think he was pretending to cope, perhaps trying to ease my pain. I didn't know what he was doing to relieve himself of that pain. Was he drinking or smoking again? It was time for both of us to get rid of the pain, no matter the risk.

So, I went back to India, settled my affairs, and told everyone I was going back to the United States to be with my husband. A lot of questions were raised. But as I have done before, I didn't feel the need to explain. In the fall of 2018, I returned to Iowa. This time, for good. Pravin was happy. He promised me we could try for another baby. I promised myself I wouldn't think of the one we'd lost.

The love of my life and our darling daughter were together under one roof, in one city, on one continent. That's how I remember 2019. A happy memory.

2019, the year we were a family again!

Soon, good news followed. I was pregnant again. This assured me that I could stay with Pravin for at least a year. We were happy, but fully aware of the reality of our situation. My life truly belonged in India. Sooner or later, I'd have to go back. We chose not to think about it. No more worries.

Until it began to hit us that something was wrong with Ishanvi.

Chapter 3: The Big Gesture

My mind began to play games. "I'm overthinking. She's fine. But what if I'm not?"

Everyone I knew was disappointed by my big gesture. I'd given up my settled life to be with my husband, and my decision had blindsided them all. I'd been settling down well in New Delhi, bought a house, arranged a reliable nanny for Ishanvi and was doing so well at work I was due for a promotion.

Was I really blinded by love? Maybe. I'm known to love fiercely.

It was hard for friends and family to understand why I'd leave a perfectly settled life for one that came with numerous "ifs" and "buts." They didn't need to understand. They didn't know that I pined to be with my husband every moment of every day or that he was struggling to be happy. They didn't know my daughter was getting used to not having her father around. They didn't understand that as a family, we were in pain.

When life gives you a hard time, you struggle to find respite, a solution that will end the misery. I thought the solution was to get my family back together and keep it that way. My life would be in order, and I could focus on mothering my daughter.

If I had only known that a bigger struggle was right around the corner.

I was so focused on the new life we were starting in America, the excitement. I didn't realize that Ishanvi wasn't speaking fluently. She was almost two-and-a-half years old.

How did I miss that?

People would say I got busy, I was careless, I was drowned in work. The truth is, I didn't know. I'm not stupid, but I didn't grow up around children. I only knew what I read in books. Ishanvi passed all the major developmental milestones on time. I had a checklist, and she checked all the boxes.

Like all parents, we were guilty of assuming that our child would turn out to be special. A dangerous cocktail of genetics and pride. Pravin and I came from different genetic pools, which we thought increased the probability that our child would be talented. Being a parent can blind you with love. Pride takes precedence over everything, and you hope for the best outcome. You want your child to be worthy of recognition. Guilty as charged!

Ishanvi was a very healthy baby. Her chubby cheeks and precious smile garnered attention wherever we went as a family. Every week, I posted a picture of her on social media and friends adored her from a distance. All was going well. She was smart, too. At eighteen months, she already knew all her letters and numbers.

During the summer of 2018, we celebrated my birthday on historic Mackinac Island, Michigan. Pravin introduced me to travel back in college, and I'm eternally grateful. It connected us as partners, and we were thrilled that Ishanvi enjoyed it too. We'd been warned that we wouldn't be able to travel as much with a baby. Ishanvi proved that wrong.

Mackinac is a gorgeous island on Lake Huron, near Michigan's upper peninsula. While we were waiting for the ferry back to the mainland, I tried to keep Ishanvi busy and Pravin held our place in the queue. I was having trouble keeping her steady, which I assumed was the case with most toddlers. Finally, I found a place worthy of her attention, a whiteboard with random numbers written on it. She pointed at the board and correctly read every number, even the double-digits. She was not even two years old.

On the ride back to our hotel, I told Pravin proudly that our daughter was special. I didn't know she was a different kind of special.

Not yet.

Chapter 4: A Mistake

nd of the year, 2018

E I was back in Iowa with Pravin. We decided to put Ishanvi in day care to help her with socialization. Midwestern winters can be brutal in a lot of ways. You can't plan outdoor activities until late spring, and we didn't want her to suffer because of the change in our living situation. She started going to day care for half a day, five days a week.

Day care was a good idea, but we chose the wrong facility, and I still blame myself for putting her through that. Pravin is a simple person. He sees the world differently than I do. We toured ten different facilities, as I insisted (thorough research) and he preferred the one with maximum diversity among the children. He thought the exposure would humble her. I fully supported him. It didn't.

It traumatized her.

She was the only child of Indian origin in that school, but I didn't expect that to be an issue. I found out later that the teachers worked at very low salaries there, which might have led to low spirits and lack of responsibility. They paid no attention to her. After a month, I asked her teacher for an update and was told she almost didn't realize Ishanvi was in her class.

"She is so quiet and easy to manage," the teacher said.

At this point, I was pregnant and throwing up every hour, so I didn't have the energy to analyze the teacher's statement, and I ignored it. I thought Ishanvi just needed time to adjust and I let it go.

I shouldn't have.

Pravin was traveling every week, Monday to Thursday, so it was my responsibility to drop Ishanvi off at school and pick her up. But I still didn't know how to drive.

The first trimester of my pregnancies had been nightmares. I couldn't sleep or eat. This time, I couldn't get out of bed, and I had another child to care for. I didn't have the strength to make her a freshly cooked meal, so she survived on prepackaged snacks. It got so bad that for one whole week, I couldn't drop her at school. I didn't think it was a big deal until I received a call.

After a week, I got a call from her day care asking why she continuously missed school. I told them I didn't have the energy to take her there, explaining my morning sickness and my lack of help. The truth is, immigrants don't take those calls lightly. I felt judged and was alarmed. The next morning, I gathered as much strength as I could and used an Uber to drop her off. When I got home, I puked for fifteen minutes. I thought that at least they wouldn't call me again. After I puked, I thought about that call again, and I'd taken it as a sign they cared.

It wasn't. What followed was even worse.

The baby was arriving that summer, and I had my hands full. Since I had established that the school cared enough to call, we decided to increase her day care hours. They didn't offer a half day tuition, so we were already paying for a full day. We might as well use those hours.

That summer, she was assigned to a new teacher whom I liked. But we ignored all the other signs. She was being bullied and didn't have the language to tell us. To this day, those nine months remain the worst time of my life as a mother. I can't forgive myself for worrying more about the baby I was carrying in my womb compared to the child who was running around. Pravin deliberately traveled that summer so he could be at home when the baby arrived. I had no family in the States and no friends. I'd never needed anyone but Pravin before this. That is the moment when I realized the price of being an immigrant. I thought I'd opted for a better life, but without a community, was it really a life?

As I dropped Ishanvi off at school in August 2019, I witnessed her getting bullied. It was serious. Maybe it was the hormones or the heat, but I'd had enough. I told Pravin we were changing her day care.

Almost as a stroke of luck, I got a call from the preschool at a local university. They had an opening. We'd liked their facility the most during our tour the year before. It was a small school. primarily catering to the children of students and teachers who attended the university. I didn't think twice before accepting.

When she started at this new school, I sighed with relief.

Three weeks later, I gave birth to her little brother, Bivan.

My struggle as a mother began again.

Chapter 5: The Birth

When Ishanvi turned three, we planned an elaborate trip to the Wild West. It had already become our tradition to travel during her birthday week.

The first year, we took her to Disneyland because she was our little princess and we wanted to express that through the Disney experience. The following year, she and I were living in India, so we visited her dad in the States, then we all went to Alaska together. She was into marine animals and bears and Pravin wanted to go somewhere far from Iowa. That was the farthest he could fly with his visa restrictions. On her third birthday, I was seven months pregnant, and she was still into animals. She'd begun to love bison, so I immediately thought of Yellowstone National Park.

I made an ambitious plan. It would be our last grand trip before we became a family of four. I decided we'd visit Yellowstone, the Grand Tetons, and Glacier National Park, all in ten days.

I'm a planner by nature. I love doing research. Planning our annual trip is my favorite thing, and I put my heart and soul into it. When we made the trip, and I saw the faces of Pravin and Ishanvi experiencing what I'd imagined, I was overwhelmed with satisfaction.

But that year, I had other worries. When we visited the pediatrician, I expressed my concerns about her shyness and speech issues. That is when we heard the word for the first time. He said the word that would eventually shake our world: autism. And he suggested we take her for testing. The idea of having a kid with a disability seemed too much for my pregnant body. I wasn't ready.

But then you never are.

We were wait-listed for testing at a reputable hospital on the University of Iowa campus in Iowa City. For a few days, Pravin and I discussed what might be wrong with her. Then he brought me back to reality. He told me to prepare for her birthday trip and the birth of our son. He wanted to distract me from thinking about Ishanvi. It didn't work, but full marks for trying.

The birthday trip went well. We explored the mountains and delighted Ishanvi with the sight of lots of bison. From the geysers of Yellowstone to the waterfalls of Glacier National Park, it was the perfect change of scenery for me. But we also saw some alarming signs.

During the trip, Ishanvi had a tantrum that lasted half an hour. It was hard to calm her down. Many more followed, and they became stronger day by day.

It was clearly a sign of something she was unable to communicate with us through words. She was frustrated, saying things we could hardly understand. A month after we returned, we got a call from her school. They wanted to discuss some of her behaviors.

My heart sank.

Before our meeting, the school emailed me about the delay in her speech. They'd hired a consultant, a former speech therapist who had previously worked for the state for more than thirty years. We knew Ishanvi would be in good hands, so we agreed to start speech therapy immediately.

Because she'd turned three, the state authorities called to ask if we'd like to have her evaluated for an Individualized Education Plan. They said she could qualify for services that would help with her speech and other issues. We began learning words that had never been part of our vocabulary.

But I still wasn't ready to think she was different or had a disability.

After dinner on September 20, 2019, we were getting ready for bed. My mother-in-law had arrived from Nepal shortly after Labor Day weekend to help with the baby's arrival. Unfortunately, Ishanvi was not very attached to her. In our culture, co-sleeping is highly encouraged. She was still sleeping with me, hands wrapped around me like she'd never let go. I knew I wouldn't be able to manage both her and the baby, so I wanted her to transition to sleeping with her grandmother, but every day she became more difficult. When she wanted me to sing a particular song but couldn't tell me which one, she screamed for forty-five minutes, until I figured out which song it was. This and other incidents gave Pravin some clarity. But I still wasn't ready.

That night, Pravin struggled to put her to bed. Falling asleep had always been an issue for her, and at times, I wasn't able to sleep for more than an hour myself. I let her sleep late in the mornings, although I myself had to get up. I thought she needed the sleep more than I did. I knew that Pravin had gone to sleep much later that particular night, because I could hear her giggling on the other side of the wall as I lay in my bed.

My contractions began at about eleven. With Ishanvi, my water had broken before I had serious contractions, and I endured twenty-two hours of labor. Knowing that Pravin might have just slept only a couple hours and that going to the hospital would mean leaving Ishanvi alone with her grandmother, I decided not to wake anyone up. I was surprised how much you learn to put your family before your own pain.

Or does that only happen to women?

I never thought I could quietly endure the pain of labor without waking anyone.

I began to time my contractions, as the doctor had taught me to do. I recited Hanuman Chalisa, a religious chant and a prayer about the Hindu god, Hanuman, who is supposed to rescue us from bad situations. My situation wasn't particularly bad, but it was extremely painful.

My mother-in-law sensed something was wrong. As I struggled to keep up with the contractions and put on a brave face, the pain increased exponentially. Pravin woke up to my screams.

"She is ready to have the baby," said my mother-in-law.

As if her words had sent a message to my baby, my water broke all over the bathroom floor. I needed to change my clothes, but I couldn't think clearly. The contractions seemed determined to kill me. Pravin helped me dress and took our hospital bag. Before leaving, I kissed Ishanvi who was sleeping peacefully in her bed, not knowing that by the time she woke up, her world would be forever changed. I gave instructions to my mother-in-law, trying to suppress my pain. "Just let her be when she wakes up. Don't make her angry. Give her lots of treats. Take her out for a walk. Don't go too far. The last time you gave me a heart attack!"

Pravin reminded me it was time to think about the other child who was desperate to be born at any moment. I always thought I would be a decent mother, never favoring one kid over the other, but it's hard. How do you decide which one needs your time and attention the most? How can you be sure they both get the love they need?

It took us five minutes to reach the hospital, but I was in excruciating pain, so it seemed much longer. The nurse offered to take me to an observation room before deciding if it was time to go to the delivery room. That was the standard procedure. I pulled her close to me and screamed, "Its fucking time!" She didn't listen and performed the observation anyway. She put her fingers inside me and said, "I can feel his head. I think he'll be here in the next few minutes."

"I told you that already!" I screamed as I was being rolled into the delivery room. Screaming made me feel better. When we passed the nurse's station, I saw how unconcerned they were, and I felt relieved. I could scream as loud as I liked.

I was suffering in the middle of the night in a small hospital in a sleepy town. When I saw my husband's face, I thought I must be dying. I knew him well enough to know why his face looked like that. He didn't think I could bear the pain, at least not without medication. I am notorious for being scared of even the slightest pain. Labor pain is the mother (pun intended) of all pains. How would I survive?

"Give her something for the pain!" he shouted.

"I'm afraid we don't have the time, Mr. Singh," the nurse replied.

The doctor arrived a minute later, and I begged her, "Please give me something for the pain. I won't survive this. If you don't believe me, look at my husband's face."

She smiled at me without answering. She seemed like a wise woman, probably in her fifties. That night she'd been waiting for her shift to end. She later told me that she was about to retire, not expecting to be needed. Instead, she decided to stay a little longer, just in case. I'm glad she didn't leave.

She directed the nurse to get the laughing gas equipment. There was no time to give me an epidural. When Pravin called the hospital from home to inform them that we were coming, I was screaming at him to tell them to get the epidural ready. I thought I'd be welcomed with an injection as soon as we walked in the door. That didn't happen.

"Time to push!" the doctor said.

"Time to push," Pravin repeated. "It's going to be okay."

I tried my best. But I couldn't push.

They kept encouraging me. In two pushes, he was out.

I didn't even have an IV or saline. During Ishanvi's birth, I'd spent twenty hours tied to a machine that constantly monitored her heartbeat as well as mine. This time, all I had were Pravin's hands firmly holding my hand and head. The nurse returned with the laughing gas equipment. It was no longer needed.

The funny thing is I'd always wanted to give birth in a place with good hospitals. I'd grown up in the nineties watching movies where the mother dies in childbirth. I didn't want to die, at least not that young. America seemed like a good place, with the best medical facilities in the world. Surely, American women didn't suffer in childbirth. That had to be one of the differences between living in a developing country and a developed one. But I was wrong. I gave birth to my son in a small rural town with no fancy medical equipment.

Bivan weighed seven pounds. Less than his sister, but he was perfect. He was beautiful. Our family was complete.

Almost immediately, I thought of Ishanvi and was surprised that I hadn't thought of her for the past few hours. That was the answer to my question. A mother prioritizes. She knows which of her children needs attention most. She does her best.

A couple of hours later, Bivan was latched onto my breast, but he was having a hard time sucking or even breathing. When I pointed that out to the nurse, she took him away.

"Just routine tests. He'll back with you soon," she said smiling. He wasn't.

They shifted him to the neonatal ICU two floors below me, and I couldn't hold him again for four days.

Chapter 6: The Hospital

September 21, 2019

Bivan had officially entered the world, but perhaps the world wasn't ready to welcome him.

After they took him for testing, I fell asleep, while Pravin went home to freshen up and check on Ishanvi. When I woke up, he was back, and talking to someone on the phone. We have relatives all over India and Nepal. The phone was our only way of telling everyone we had a new member of the family. He was smiling as he was talking, probably with his sister Nidhi.

The nurse came in and wanted our attention. She said the doctor would come and talk to us in detail but as of now, Bivan would remain in neonatal intensive care. The words "intensive care" sent shivers down my spine. "Was he okay?"

She wouldn't tell me anything.

The doctor, a neonatal pediatrician, arrived soon after and explained that Bivan couldn't breathe properly and was on oxygen support. As I struggled to fight my tears and ask all the right questions, he told us there was nothing to worry about. Our baby was being monitored, and they were running more tests to find out if there was a bigger issue.

All I heard was "a bigger issue," and "not able to breathe." I couldn't breathe properly myself. Pravin held my hands as we watched the doctor walk away, closing the door behind him.

We were alone, and I didn't know what he was thinking.

We were silent for a minute.

"He's going to be fine," Pravin said. "I'll ask mother to stay with you tonight."

It was a good idea. Another mother would know what to do, or at least, give me the support I needed. He left that evening and came back with a surprise.

As they opened the door, Ishanvi ran in and hugged me.

"Mama!" That word brought me relief that I hadn't thought was even possible.

Pravin has always known how to cheer me up. It's one of the biggest reasons why I love him so much.

My mother-in-law seemed a bit worried, quite visibly. Pravin must have filled her in on the baby. It must have been hard for her, as well. She would have wanted to see the baby. In her culture, the boys always get more attention than the girls, and grandsons are cherished. I'd been so worried about telling them our firstborn was a girl I almost didn't mention it when we found out.

Female infanticide is a real issue in some parts of India. Families have such a strong preference for boys, the mothers are forced to abort if they find out it's a girl, so divulging the sex of a fetus is prohibited. Even thinking about it, bothers me. I want to scream at those people!

But Pravin's parents are a godsend. They have evolved so elegantly that I sometimes can't believe my luck. They never cared that our first child was a girl. They were just happy we were having a baby.

While Ishanvi cuddled me like she hadn't seen me for days, the phone rang.

A call from the NICU.

"You can come see him if you'd like."

I was finally happy. All four of us set out to visit Bivan.

I had never been to an NICU before, but the moment I entered, I realized it was a special place. Life is a struggle, but those babies are being forced to experience that from the moment of birth or even earlier. They had to be fighters. That's how I wanted to see my son. A fighter, a survivor.

As we passed several families and their precious babies, I sensed a heavy energy. There had to be. It was a battlefield. Those babies were fighting to earn a place in this world. We found Bivan in a small crib almost at the back of the room. Tubes were attached to his nose and feet, and he was wearing a tiny blue hat and an open front onesie, sleeping peacefully, oblivious that so many people loved him dearly. He wouldn't be able to meet some of them for a long time.

His area was well lit, furnished with a zoo-themed nightlight and a rocking chair. Pravin's mom went to him, took a close look, and said, "He has the perfect nose!"

I figured she was proud. Her family includes some of the prettiest people I've ever seen, beginning with her. When we met, Pravin had perfect cheekbones, and his sister Nidhi is the epitome of untouched beauty. Pravin diluted his good genes by marrying me, an outsider, not even from his caste. I liked that his mother was proud of her grandson's nose and that it promised a good face. It didn't mean she would have loved him less had that been otherwise.

Ishanvi couldn't understand what was happening. She stood close to me, and instead of looking at the baby, got distracted by the night lamp. It had animal statues all around it. She loved animals, after all, and she was only three years old. Just like I understood her grandmother, I understood her. They both had their reasons.

The pediatrician arrived, also with a smile. He said the tests indicated some sort of infection, and until they knew what it was and treated it, Bivan would have to stay in the NICU for at least three days. I would be discharged the next day. How exactly would that work?

"You can give us your milk supply. We'll be sure to feed him that instead of baby formula. You're welcome to feed him yourself if you'd like."

He had seen the question on my face. Babies can feed seven times a day. It would be impossible for me to always be there to feed him.

"We'll figure something out," Pravin said. I believed him. We always do.

The next morning, I was discharged without the baby. I'd imagined leaving the hospital with my son, my mother-in-law eagerly waiting to perform traditional Hindu welcome rituals.

There were no welcome rituals but a super elated Ishanvi.

However, I constantly worried about the baby. I told Pravin I'd like to stay at the hospital at night in case the baby needed me. At the NICU, I'd befriended a kind nurse who told me about a room in the unit I could use to get some rest. She said she'd wake me up whenever the baby woke up. I didn't know then that kind and caring people like her would help me survive for a long time to come.

Pravin agreed without arguing. One of the perks of being a mother who couldn't bring her baby home from the hospital. I played with Ishanvi as much as I could, trying to make up for lost time, but I knew that time, once lost, is gone forever.

I had dinner and went back to the hospital with Pravin, leaving a crying Ishanvi with her grandmother. She couldn't understand why I had to go back so soon, and I couldn't explain it to her. My other baby needed me more. A mother's priorities.

Chapter 7: The Appointment

After I was discharged, I managed to visit the hospital for two nights. I'd spend time with Ishanvi after she got home from school, feed her dinner, then leave to feed my other baby. I was happy to do it, but I was tired all the time because I couldn't get enough sleep. It was what motherhood entailed for me at the time, and I accepted it. I realized I was much stronger than I'd thought. I was finally becoming a strong mother.

Every night, the hospital staff greeted me with a smile, especially the nurses. It must be such a tiring job, watching those beautiful babies struggle to survive. But they did it effortlessly, day in and day out. One of the nurses told me that the further your baby's room is from the NICU entrance, the greater danger he's in. Within two days, Bivan was moved closer to the entrance. My prayers seemed to be working.

On the third day when I arrived at the hospital, they checked my temperature and told me I had a fever. They refused to let me see him. Stupid hospital protocols. It was heartbreaking to be that close yet unable to hold him. Pravin fed him from a bottle as I waited impatiently outside.

He came back with the empty bottle, smiling. "He sure is eating well!" As usual, my husband was trying to look on the bright side, but I couldn't see my baby. A bright side didn't exist.

When I came home, Ishanvi was delighted. One baby's loss was another's gain. In the morning, I realized that my body had needed a full night's sleep. I didn't even wake up to pump, and I felt refreshed, although my breasts were leaking.

I pumped the milk, had my coffee, and got Ishanvi ready for school. When I called the NICU, I was told that I would be able to hold my baby again after my temperature had been normal for twenty-four hours. That meant I'd have to wait at least another day.

After Ishanvi left for school, Pravin asked me if I'd like to do something. I didn't feel like it, but I knew I had to keep my mind occupied. To keep myself busy, I started preparing for the baby's arrival. The doctor had told me that he wouldn't be home for at least a week. I'd imagined he'd be back with me by now, resting in his crib. It wasn't fair, but I knew better than to expect fairness. Life is meant to be a mess. It makes it dynamic, but when you're in the middle of the mess, you can't understand that. It only becomes clear after you've regained control of the situation and can step back to see the full picture.

Ishanvi's school called. They wanted to talk. I figured it was about her behavior.

With the hospital visits and fear for my newborn son, I'd forgotten about Ishanvi's issues. I realized how difficult it must have been for Pravin and his mother to manage her without me.

Pravin and I had lunch while I told him about the call from her school, and he agreed to go. I insisted on coming with him.

"You just gave birth," he said. "You need to recover."

"I will, eventually. But I need to get back on my feet for my daughter."

Pravin smiled. His eyes told me he knew I was back. I handed him my notes about what to discuss with her teachers. That is how I knew I was back!

For the next two days, Parvin visited the hospital while I stayed home with Ishanvi. I was waiting to feel better and trying to spend as much time with her as I could because I knew things wouldn't be the same once her brother was home. She didn't have the slightest idea that her life was about to change. She never asked about the baby she'd met at the hospital, and I wondered if she knew who he was. She wasn't even curious.

The meeting at her school was on a Thursday, five days after Bivan's birth. The doctors had told us Bivan might be out of danger and ready to come home by the weekend, and I was feeling positive. I dressed properly for the first time since I'd come back from the hospital. Nurses and doctors are in scrubs all day, so they don't judge their patients' attire. I assumed they didn't care. But I wanted to look nice for Ishanvi's school.

A few weeks before Ishanvi was born, Pravin surprised me with a beautiful red Volkswagen Passat. We did little things to make memories. We took numerous trips with her in that car, from Niagara Falls when she was just two months old, Grandma keeping her company in the backseat, to South Dakota, her first long drive with me and Pravin. For her first birthday, we drove to Florida, and for her fourth birthday, to the Upper Peninsula of Michigan.

That day, as I sat in the car, lost in thought, Pravin looked behind me. The car seat was empty, and that brought a slight ache to my heart. I'd been getting a lot of those lately, probably a side effect of motherhood.

When we entered the school, the team was waiting for us. Ms. Amy, her classroom teacher, greeted us with a smile. She was a beautiful, kind Midwesterner with great passion for her work, and her energy was infectious. She'd visited us before the school accepted Ishanvi and we'd shared stories.

Mrs. Jager, a retired social worker and the school consultant, smiled and introduced herself. She looked old enough to be wiser than anyone I'd ever met. We were seated in a small basement room away from the classrooms. As the noise of the kids faded, I could hear my heartbeat getting louder. What did they want to talk about?

We were welcomed, and the team was introduced. Someone said they were there to help. I could feel it. That was positive enough for me.

"You have a wonderful daughter. So sensitive and kind."

My heart swelled.

"But we've noticed that she has some peculiar challenges."

The ache came rushing back.

For fifteen minutes, they described the "peculiar" behaviors Ishanvi exhibited. She froze while doing a task. She was unable to follow basic directions. She lacked social interaction.

When I heard "lack of social interaction," I thought of David, a little guy whose eyes lit up the minute he saw her enter the classroom. No matter what he was doing, he hurried to greet her. Ishanvi never responded to him. She was shy, that's what we always thought. But the teachers were saying it might be more than shyness.

After half an hour, Mrs. Jager reluctantly said, "Maybe it's time to look into other possibilities, such as autism."

Pravin broke the silence. "We're already wait-listed for testing at the University of Iowa."

She sighed loudly out of relief.

"I cannot tell you how many times in my career I've dreaded the parents' reaction when I tell them to consider autism."

"Is it that bad?" Pravin asked.

"Oh, yes. I've always had a negative reaction, often driven by emotion. Your reaction is one I will remember for a long time. You were cool as a cucumber."

Pravin smiled. It wasn't a happy smile. "You and I are on the same team with a common goal of helping my daughter. Why would I be offended if you suspect she has challenges that could mean she's autistic?"

"Not a lot of parents think like that."

"I want what's best for my child. If she's autistic, she'll need all the help in the world, and that starts with a diagnosis. Your advice takes me a step closer to figuring out what's going on in that little head of hers."

We all smiled. For an introvert who has trouble framing sentences when he's not at work, Pravin did great.

I thought, "We'll survive this with him by my side."

Chapter 8: Homecoming

That weekend, we brought Bivan home. I was elated. My little boy was out of NICU and danger. I thanked the nurses and kept the list of their names in the little box of memories I made for each of my children. They had helped him survive his first week on Earth, and when he's old enough to understand, I'll tell him about them.

Ishanvi's box contains her "birthday girl" badge from Disneyland and the rocks we collected during her subsequent birthday trips—from Lake Superior in Michigan to Lake McDonald in Montana.

Bivan's box contains his hospital name tag and the list of NICU nurses. He has just started his journey, and I'm sure I'll add more treasures.

I imagine rummaging through these items when I'm old, my memory already weakened, unable to remember their relevance. Maybe my kids will help me remember and cherish the little moments that made up their lives. It will be my way of holding on to the memories a little longer. I wish I had a way to stop time and enjoy some moments a little longer. Time seems cruel that way.

That weekend, I decided to forget about our meeting with the school. I wanted to celebrate Bivan's homecoming. So, I prepared a good meal to showcase my excitement. After I'd finished cooking, my mother-in-law decided to tell me that I was supposed to stay out of the kitchen for fourteen days after the delivery. Hindu rituals. She said she hadn't had the heart to tell me before, seeing how excited I was. I was grateful she'd let me be. Sometimes that's the kindest thing you can do for someone.

For the first few days after Bivan came home, we were extra careful with him. I believe that was a normal reaction from parents who've seen their babies tied up with tubes. We couldn't help wondering if he'd be okay without them. Ishanvi's behavior didn't help.

She liked the idea of a brother at the hospital. I didn't know how to tell her that he was home for good, but I think she figured out a way to cope. She started watching an Indian cartoon series on Netflix called *Chhota Bheem* and often called the main character "baby." We tried everything. We'd say, "Look, baby brother." She'd point to the television saying, "That is baby," and jump around the couch.

It was funny at times, but also concerning. We wondered why it was so hard for her to see her baby brother and worried that she'd never accept him.

Pravin's mom worried, too, but we had bigger fish to fry. In a few months, our US visas would expire, and if our Green Card didn't arrive in time, we'd have to leave the country. It was a tough time, dealing with a newborn, a child who might have special needs, and the uncertainty of our residency.

I suppose a lot of immigrant families go through this phase, not knowing what's in store for them, at the mercy of the US immigration system. Our lawyers assured us there was a good chance things would fall into place. We are law-abiding residents and we followed the due process. So, we decided to move to Naperville, Illinois, in the western suburbs of Chicago. It had been long considered one of the best cities in US to raise a family, with excellent schools and the best public library system in the country. We thought if we were to live in America permanently, we should find a city that would make it worth it.

But March 2020 brought dark times. The world was dealing with a deadly pandemic. I was so stressed; I was losing sleep. Bivan wasn't letting me sleep, anyway. My relationship with Pravin was suffering.

And before we moved to Naperville, something happened.

Chapter 9: The Diagnosis

A few weeks after Bivan was born, we got a call from the University of Iowa's campus in Davenport where we'd been wait-listed. They had an opening and could test Ishanvi. Pravin had an important work commitment on the day they proposed. I still couldn't drive but didn't want to miss the appointment. I told him I'd take a cab. It would be expensive, and Davenport can be a dangerous town. Pravin was worried about our safety and my mother-in-law worried about feeding the baby in my absence.

I told Pravin I'd be on call so he could be sure we were safe. I'd pump milk for Bivan, and if it ran out, my mother-in-law could feed him formula. By then, I'd realized I could find solutions to my problems if I prioritized and thought them through. That day, my priority was Ishanvi.

As soon as we got into the cab, I started making conversation with the driver. I figured if he knew me, he wouldn't be tempted to harm me. He turned out to be a nice fellow. I texted Pravin, "All good. Driver seems nice."

"Okay. Good. Keep me posted," he replied.

Ishanvi was happily looking out the window at the clouds, pretending they formed animal shapes. I looked at her with both hope and despair, wondering where the journey would take us.

The answer was "nowhere." At least not until a few months later. The doctor sadly informed me that Ishanvi was too shy and quiet to be tested. The results would be inconclusive. She never mentioned autism. Instead, she recommended private speech therapy.

"At least we can start private speech therapy," Pravin told me sensing my disappointment.

"Also, now I know I don't need you to take me everywhere if I have enough money to pay for a cab."

Deep down, I felt he should have been with me that day, but I understood that he would have driven us if he could. We always understand one another.

In January 2020, as we were preparing to move to Naperville, Ishanvi's autism test was rescheduled. The hospital had enquired if she was making progress with speech therapy, and we happily confirmed that she was. She could be tested for autism and the results would be conclusive. Her speech had improved tremendously, but my heart was still in pain.

For days before her tests, I struggled with anxiety, I thought it was postpartum hormones, but there were other factors. We were moving to a new city, knowing that we might have to leave the country soon. To say that I had a lot on my plate would be an understatement.

On January 31, 2020, the doctors at the University of Iowa confirmed that Ishanvi had autism spectrum disorder.

I felt we'd been hit by a storm and didn't know where to find shelter. It took us a while to regroup and figure out the next steps.

I remember the struggle, the questions, the anger immediately following the diagnosis. But I also remember that we were there for each other as a family. More importantly, we were prepared for anything. Pravin reminded me that we had been through a lot as teenagers. We'd had to grow up before our time, so we had resilience. We'd get over whatever we were feeling. But getting that diagnosis for your child hits hard, no matter what.

If you're a mother, father, sibling, or grandparent who is emotionally attached to the kid, the news is extremely difficult to digest. I believe we went through phases similar to grief—disbelief, anger, sadness, and sometimes, all those emotions at once.

Years later, I read my kids a book by Diane Alber called *A Little Spot of Feelings and Emotions*. The protagonist is tangled in all the emotions combined and doesn't know how to separate his feelings. Right after the diagnosis, I felt like that.

Once I made peace with the diagnosis, days of research followed. Knowledge brought calmness. I'd been the school nerd, so at a very young age I'd learned that many resources are available. First, I needed to help myself, clear my head and create a vision for my daughter. It was challenging, because autism is still under extensive research, and there's a lack of awareness. I didn't know much about it myself. When I heard "autism" I thought of the film *Rain Man* starring Tom Cruise and Dustin Hoffman or the Bollywood movie *Barfi* starring Priyanka Chopra. The internet was full of myths about the causes and effects of autism. It was difficult to navigate, but we prevailed. We had to. For Ishanvi.

I began meeting families with special needs kids, and my heart suffered when I realized that although our journeys were different, we all wanted the best for our kids, and we were all worried.

I started reading books and following social media accounts that promised to give me some knowledge.

There are things I wish I had known when she was first diagnosed. Things I wish I'd done better. But I know time teaches us differently. All I can do now is learn from my mistakes and, if possible, pass on my learning to families who are fighting the same battle.

I became introspective and documented some of my feelings, realizing I was in new territory. I'd never know everything about autism. I tried. But it was too much. I joined a support group, but found the experience too emotional, and soon realized that the journey was my own to take.

I was surprised to see changes in myself. I'd begun to learn and evolve. Soon, I started telling other families about these lessons. I interacted with families in India as well as the US. It was liberating to know that my journey, although unique, was in some ways like that of other parents. And I believe I helped them.

Slowly, I recognized the power of storytelling. When we share our journeys through stories, we help others believe we're all human beings who experience varying levels of grief and joy. To think that we're alone would be a huge error. We are all in this together. I wanted to scream that to families with special needs kids, because I hadn't heard it clearly when I started my journey.

Eventually, I developed the nine best life lessons I'd learned as the parent of an autistic girl. I wish I'd known them before, but I don't have any regrets. I'm proud of the kind, caring human Ishanvi is becoming. We all wonder about the future, but all we can do is work on the present to ensure that the future is better and brighter. I always say, "Enjoy the present before it becomes the past."

I analyzed my story and devised a philosophy of living a happy and fruitful life. Every parent can refer to these lessons, especially if they have a special needs kid.

Parenting is hard, and it doesn't come with a handbook. I learned most things on the job. But I look back and think of all the steps I took, the barriers I overcame, and all the wonderful people I met because of Ishanvi.

I followed a nine-step process, which I believe will help both the children and their caregivers. I call it "A New Beginning."

There's no denying that life takes a different turn when someone you love has special needs. What we can control is how soon we make ourselves worthy of that life. You don't have to give birth to a special needs child to benefit from these strategies. They can help anyone understand the struggle of parents like me. To be empathetic, kind, and aware is a way of building a better future together.

Shweta and I connected through a group of suburban women who meet once a month for healthy conversations. We became dear friends, and she shared that she often questioned why she'd been chosen to mother a kid on the spectrum. She'd struggled with it for a while, but once she'd answered that question, she was prepared to move on and help her child. She said she realized she was a chosen one, that it was a blessing because only she had the strength to do it. I applaud her thinking every day. We often talk about how hard it is to manage our kids. But we gather strength from each other and our stories and move on because our precious kids need us.

For the last two and a half years, I've followed these nine simple steps. inspired by my own experience and the experiences of other parents. I believe by following these steps, I became the best version of myself as a parent.

Prepare-Stop-Accept-Focus-Highlight-Be Kind-Enjoy-Embrace-Celebrate

THESE STEPS CHANGED my perspective on life.

While I was documenting my journey with Ishanvi, I was helping myself in ways I hadn't yet imagined. I began with the intention of helping parents like me, but realized I needed it more than anyone. My struggles, after all, won't end.

PART 2
The Lessons

Lesson 1: Prepare for a Challenging Life.

Ishanvi was a physically normal baby. I had a normal pregnancy. Pravin was living in the US, and I was in India, so I traveled a lot, but it never bothered us. We're connected by love, willing to do anything to make our family work.

Our daughter completed all her milestones on time and was a happy baby. At eighteen months, I took her to New Delhi where I was working as deputy manager of a government firm. I left her at home with a nanny all day and came back to a happy child playing on her own. She loved toys. She still does.

My husband and I are both qualified engineers. We dated for seven years before getting married and waited another four before having Ishanvi. The thought of a child blessed with genes from our two cultures excited us. We had some idea of genetics and knew there was a high probability that she'd be exceptionally intelligent.

When she was born, we thought we were right. She amazed us every step of the way. At eighteen months, she could identify her numbers and recite the alphabet. No puzzle was too hard for her to solve in minutes. Sometimes she'd hold a puzzle board upside down, while she completed it. That was her way of telling us she wanted a challenge. Amidst all this excitement, we overlooked an important factor. She wasn't really interacting with us. Because we traveled back and forth from the US to India, we didn't have a steady circle of friends. So, she never really identified with a social group. But that never bothered us. We were happy with the way things were going.

I overlooked the red flags. When I took her to Kathmandu, Nepal for a family wedding, she was uncomfortable with people congregating to see her. She was the first grandchild on my husband's side, and his relatives were eager to meet her. I couldn't prevent them from showering her with love. She deserved it. But she didn't like it. We needed to respect that, but I didn't know she was overstimulated. I didn't even know what that word meant.

Whenever someone approached her, she began to scream. I couldn't leave her for a second, so I had to leave early. I was harshly judged for it, but the only opinion I cared about was my husband's. Unfortunately, he didn't understand either. He'd been unable to come to Kathmandu because of visa restrictions, so it was important that our daughter and I were there.

He asked, "What's the issue? Why can't you pacify your own daughter?"

I didn't have an answer. Not then. I wanted to tell people it was hard for me to understand Ishanvi, but I was afraid I'd be judged even more harshly if I admitted it. So, I kept quiet and took all the blame. I was a bad mother. That explained it. I told Pravin that I hadn't spent enough time with Ishanvi, so I didn't know how to calm her. He didn't seem to disagree, which made me believe in it even more. I was devastated. Pravin stood with the people who pointed a finger at me. A piece of my heart broke and for a long time, I felt alone.

Sometimes Ishanvi wouldn't wear clothes she didn't feel good about. By the time she was a year old, she had a closet full of designer dresses, so I'd scream at her for being spoiled. Little did I know that she was trying to show me she was different. I wish I'd understood her more.

I felt helpless. I spent almost eight months with her in South Delhi in a big, posh, three-bedroom house. I chose to sleep in one of the smaller bedrooms, locked the door and didn't venture out at night, even for a glass of water. The grandness of the house didn't matter. I felt alone.

Sundays were the worst. On other days, I had the company of her nanny. Sometimes the nanny called me on a Sunday afternoon to ask if I needed her to come. I never had the courage to tell her that I could use company in that big house. I knew how painful it was for her to be away from her own family. I couldn't ask her to come back early unless it was an emergency.

One night during a heavy storm, the electricity went out. I don't like the dark at all. I feel suffocated. So, I hesitatingly called her cell and asked her to spend the night at my house. She happily obliged and braved the storm to obey my instructions. I'll never forget her. She is a lot more than just a nanny. She understood that I was alone, not just physically, but emotionally, as well. She often told me how much she appreciated my staying in India, because it meant she had a well-paying job. Yet she prayed that I could reunite with my husband before long. I believe her prayers were answered. After eight months of struggling with a stressful long-distance relationship, I was ready to join Pravin, leaving my job and our nanny in India.

After I moved to the US, I took time off from work and became a stay-at-home mom. I began to observe Ishanvi's behavior a little more carefully. By the time she was three, we'd had a couple incidents of unpredictable behavior, episodes when we couldn't figure out what the problem was. I pointed that out to our pediatrician at her annual physical, and he agreed we should have her evaluated.

That's when we started to get nervous. We couldn't imagine that our daughter had issues. I'd had a normal pregnancy and delivery. I'd breastfed her until I got pregnant again. She ate well and seemed to be having a happy childhood. What could possibly be wrong?

. . . .

JANUARY 30, 2020

We drove to Iowa city, ninety-minutes from our home in the Quad Cities, to have her evaluated by a team of experts at the University of Iowa Stead Family Children's Hospital. This time, Pravin accompanied me. So many things were going through my mind. What if she were autistic? Maybe it was just a matter of delayed speech. My mind played terrible games.

She was scheduled to be evaluated by a team of doctors, but halfway through the drive, we were told that one of them had cancelled. We would not be given a confirmed diagnosis, so it was recommended that we reschedule the visit. The next day, we were relocating to Naperville, Illinois, so we told them it would be impossible to make the trip again.

On the way back, Ishanvi insisted we do something fun. We pulled into a place on the I-80 that claims to be the world's largest truck stop and bought her a stuffed elephant with a cool purple hoodie. We still have that in the playroom, and whenever she plays with it, it reminds me of the day when our lives changed forever.

Back home, the hospital called us again, this time informing us they might be able to find a replacement for the missing doctor. We thought about it for a second, then started the journey again. The same thoughts rushed through my mind. I had a newborn whom I hadn't thought of once since we'd left the house that morning. As I watched her happily playing with her toy, I said a prayer and hoped there was nothing to be worried about.

The testing took four long, grueling hours. We were with her for a while, then called to a parent interview in a different room. She was showing tremendous improvement in her speech. So, the part of the test we witnessed was comforting. She seemed to be doing so well.

Finally, the entire team gave us the official diagnosis. They said they usually don't deliver the results right away, but since we were moving out of state the next day, they'd make an exception. We were grateful.

Then they just said it. She's on the spectrum. For a moment, my heart sank. Until then, there was always a chance she was perfectly normal. The news changed everything. I wondered how I could care for her without any knowledge of her condition. I sent her to day care for six hours so I could relax a bit and take care of the baby. I learned that Ishanvi has difficulty expressing herself. No one understands her. I felt terrible.

I asked if I should stop sending her to day care and take care of her at home. It sounded like she had a contagious disease. That was my lack of unawareness. I simply didn't know.

This is what the doctor replied. I still carry it with me:

"Why would you want to treat her differently? She's still the same child you brought in. You have just learned she's a bit different from others. The diagnosis is for the people around her. She knows who she is. It's your turn to know her better and treat her accordingly. She doesn't need special treatment. She just needs more understanding."

In a few sentences, she explained that we should take the diagnosis as though nothing had changed. Was it true though? No matter how pragmatic you are, it hits you hard. The drive back home was tough.

We all have turning points in our lives, moments that can change the course of our lives. For our family, that drive was one of those moments. Life as we knew it was about to change forever, and we weren't prepared. Life hadn't always been easy for us, but this challenge brought us into foreign territory. We didn't know the world of special needs kids. Not yet.

My big takeaway from that day was that life was going to be hard. It always is. We had to accept that and get ready for the challenge that lay ahead. Everyone processes news like this differently. Whatever that process may be, you need to buckle up and do everything in your power to build a happy life. The challenges will come and go, so be prepared.

An Imperfect Life

It took our family time to realize that we couldn't change the past or what was happening to us. Ishanvi's diagnosis, though hard hitting, taught us a valuable lesson. Life won't always be rosy, but we're faced with challenges so we can evolve and grow. Pravin and I figured we'd faced too many challenges to let this one dampen our spirits. Ishanvi is our little girl, the joy of our lives, our firstborn. Nothing changes that. Our life is in our hands, and it's up to us to make out of it what we will.

We started doing our research and learning more about autism spectrum disorder. We were surprised how little we knew and how much information was available. While we were educating ourselves, we realized that we needed to let Ishanvi be herself. The first thing we learned is that she's unique, not "abnormal." I hear that word constantly and I hate it. It's demeaning and unnecessary. I've met parents who want their kids to fit in, to be "normal," and I hate to admit that I don't enjoy talking to them. I wish I could tell them to change their perspective instead of pushing their kids in that way. We must celebrate our kids, especially their uniqueness.

We celebrate Ishanvi like a star. We focus on her issues but give her the freedom to be herself. We're proud of how far she's come, and we celebrate that every single day. She's as normal as life itself.

She's still our cheerful and obedient little girl. We're doing everything in our capacity to keep her that way. But in the summer of 2022, something changed. She got her first taste of ruthlessness, and so did we.

I'd decided to give her a break from therapy and enrolled her in a summer camp with neurotypical kids. She was forming connections as I'd hoped, and that brightened my spirit. But as it is with life, there will always be people who try to throw a challenge or two at you. That summer, she got a taste of unfairness.

When she turned six in July, she changed classrooms to be with the six-year-old kids. I'd asked the Park District to make an exception, since being in a new class would be another adjustment. I wasn't sure why it was needed with less than a month of classes left. But they refused. Rules were rules, they said. I accepted it as a challenge. Sadly, some of the older kids were unkind to her.

One day while I was picking her up, her counselor told me she'd been bullied. My heart sank. My first question was, "Did she retaliate?"

The answer was no.

As I seated her in our car and began the drive back home, she kept asking, "Why did he do that?" She kept referring to the bully as a friend. "Why, Mama, why?"

I couldn't hold back my tears and I began to weep, not because someone had treated her badly, but because she didn't blame the kid. She just wanted to know why he did it. I regained my composure and told her, "Because your friend was weak. Meanness is often a sign of weakness. It has nothing to do with you, dear."

She smiled. I asked her what she was thinking.

"If he forgot to be kind to me, that's okay. Tomorrow, I'll tell him to remember to be kind. I'll be responsible."

I had recently taught her the word. R-E-S-P-O-N-S-I-B-L-E.

She used it the right way, without carrying any malice in her heart. I was stunned by her innocence and my ability to handle the situation in a positive way.

My first lesson is about preparing for a difficult life. How do you do that? How do you prepare for situations like that one? How do you keep yourself from getting angry or screaming at people who treat your child differently?

The answer is simple. You make every difficult situation a lesson. You remind people to be kind.

That fall, when the school asked for art submissions for a national PTA contest, I encouraged her to use the bullying incident to create a vision with the help of an artist friend, Susmita, who owns a studio close to our community. Ishanvi created a beautiful image of happy kids and smiling flowers calling it "A world full of smiles." It was her vision of how the world should be. For the artist's statement, she narrated the incident and how it had taught her to be responsible. My mom's heart has never been prouder.

That day, I learned that my daughter is kind and forgiving, and that I'm giving her a way to channel her experiences, both good and bad, in a creative way. My hope is that this will help her navigate bigger problems in life, and that she'll remember to use it, even when I'm no longer around to remind her.

Even as adults, we make decisions about how we react to various situations. Nobody does it for us. Ishanvi's reaction and spirit that day taught me more than I've learned from any other life lesson.

Yes, life will bring challenges, but you have the power to stay calm, forgive, and move on.

So, our family moves on. That philosophy has helped us remain happy and content.

I'm often asked how I manage to stay calm, considering how difficult my life is. I deal with therapies, commitments, and a full-time job. I smile and say that my family keeps me going. I see life as an opportunity, no matter the circumstances. Why waste it overthinking and overanalyzing?

What they see as a tiring, challenging life is a fulfilling one for me. I see the glass half full.

Pravin and I have built this life together and Ishanvi and Bivan are two little blessings. Whatever life wants from me, I'm willing to give it one hundred percent. So, bring it on!

We accept every challenge head on and have built a life full of love and affection. We travel, celebrate, and stick together, making the most of what life has given us.

When Bivan turned one, we continued our tradition of traveling for the kid's birthdays and rented a beautiful house in Saugatuck, on the shore of Lake Michigan, surrounded by forests. It was the perfect getaway, but we didn't realize that the house had vaulted ceilings with fans. Ishanvi was going through an irrational fear of fans. She refused to go inside.

In an instant, our joy and excitement transformed into fear. We'd paid a good amount of money to book the house, and I had an itinerary full of fun activities, from apple picking (for the kids) to wine tasting (not for the kids).

Ishanvi found a swing on the porch and sat there rocking back and forth. I think it calmed her, because after about twenty minutes, she said, "I'm ready to go in."

Our hearts were full. She was willing to fight her fears. My brave little girl.

It was 2020. COVID had delayed my return to India, so we were still able to enjoy our life together, all four of us.

That night after putting the kids to bed, Pravin and I stood on the staircase and talked about how far we'd come as a family. What would happen if I had to go back to New Delhi for work? I didn't want to think about it.

The next morning, Pravin told me he'd found out our Green Cards had been processed. I was free to leave my job in India, and we could finally settle down in the US without the risk of being separated. In the evening, we made a bonfire and roasted marshmallows, each of us holding one of the kids. We could stay together, holding them for as long as we liked.

The next morning, we woke up early and saw that a family of deer had come to visit us. Ishanvi was overjoyed. She said she loved this vacation.

What started as a challenging situation, turned into a series of memorable moments. There's always a chance that a challenge might turn into something positive if we know how to fight it.

I often say that we have an imperfect life, but a life full of love.

When my kids look back on their childhood, I want them to remember a loving family who can be silly and fun. When Ishanvi flaps her hands in excitement, we ask Google Home to play her favorite song and we dance with her. She loves that. She flaps away.

When Bivan has a meltdown, we respect that and give him time to get past it. I want them to remember this family as a place where they felt loved, appreciated, and valued, so that one day, they'll be able to open their hearts to others. I hope that when they grow up, they'll look at everyone with kindness and love.

If they do that, I'll consider my job as a mother well done!

Lesson 2: Stop Blaming. No One Is Responsible

Day of the diagnosis

As we drove away from Iowa city, we were tired and hungry. We hadn't realized that the testing would take so long, and we were in a hurry to get home to the baby. I was breastfeeding and hadn't had time to pump, so I was leaking. It was a ninety-minute drive back to the Quad Cities, but we were feeling emotional, so it seemed longer.

Pravin and I had been together for fourteen years and we'd had our fair share of challenges, but we took comfort in knowing that we'd always been there for each other. This time, another human being was involved, a tiny one, giggling in the back seat. She had no idea what had just happened or that the visit had transformed our lives.

We were silent for a while, then Pravin said, "We knew something was wrong. It's good that we know for sure. Now we can help her."

Even when he should be sad, Pravin can say something positive and practical. I was proud of him, but I couldn't understand why he wasn't worried. Maybe because I'd just given birth to a tiny human, my hormones were acting crazy, and I wanted to cry. But I didn't want to be vulnerable in front of him when he was trying hard to stay positive for my sake.

By the time we got home, I'd made up a list of topics to research—treatment plans, schools, social life, life in general. I wanted to devote my energy to that. But I couldn't. I kept going back to the same question: "Why Ishanvi? What really happened? Did I eat something wrong, do something wrong while I carried her in my womb? It had been a stressful time for us. While I was trying to get pregnant, I'd planned to finish my master's degree in the US.

The first week of November 2015 was eventful. That Monday, I found out that I'd been accepted at the prestigious University of

Connecticut, majoring in Environmental Engineering, my dream. That Wednesday, I took a pregnancy test and discovered I was about to have a baby. Over the weekend, we found out that our visa extension had been rejected, and we'd have to return to India within ten days.

There's more!

I had mentally quit my job in India so I could be with Pravin in the States. We didn't think we'd have to go back, so we'd ended our lease in New Delhi and sold our belongings. Now we didn't have a home, and I wasn't sure I still had a job.

I had terrible morning sickness and was losing weight rapidly. Because the rules had changed, Pravin's passport was due for renewal, so he couldn't travel to India with me. Instead, he'd have to fly to his home country, Nepal.

So, there we were, on the verge of becoming parents, the best news we could receive, but we were busy figuring out how to leave the States and had no idea what the future held.

Separately, we took fourteen-hour flights.

In India, I fought for my job, settled, and bought a house. My family told me it was time we bought a house our future child could call home. I understood that they were looking out for us. This traveling out of a suitcase wasn't viable with a baby.

Till the time I finalized the home, I was staying with Manu, our college friend, and Indranee who had grown up close to my hometown. Over time, our bond strengthened. They have gone above and beyond to help us whenever we needed help, and they mean the world to me.

They lived in Noida, about an hour's drive from my job in New Delhi. I didn't know how to drive and didn't own a car, so I took cabs to work, always asking the driver to go slowly over the speed bumps to protect what was inside my growing belly.

One day, when Manu and Indranee had gone shopping, an earthquake struck. I am a survivor of Nepal earthquake of 2015 that killed more than 9000 people. Since then, I have carried trauma associated with this natural disaster. This time, it couldn't have come at a worse time. I was alone, on the sixth-floor, taking some much needed rest. Suddenly the bed starts shaking violently. Before I realized what it was, my body went into shock. But I heard screams from outside and people running towards the stairs, and my mind woke up, telling me to run! I did, one staircase at a time, continuously praying that I survive. I waited away from the buildings for about an hour, before it was time to go back. But I was not ready. A neighbor spotted me and came to my rescue, keeping me company. I think she figured out that I was too scared to go back up. She remained by my side until I gathered the courage to go back. Ironically the elevators weren't working so I had to walk the same stairs one by one. That night, I couldn't sleep.

My favorite Hindi movie, *Barfi,* is the heartwarming story of the love between an autistic girl and a nonverbal boy. During my pregnancy, I watched it again. When we got Ishanvi's diagnosis, I wondered if that had been a mistake. My first search on Google was "causes of autism." There is no definitive answer. Research is ongoing but inconclusive.

We might be an evolved species, but we succumb to our egos, and we're inherently curious. Why was my daughter atypical? There was no history of autism spectrum disorder in either of our families. The sooner we stopped asking that unanswerable question, the sooner we'd be ready to face the truth.

According to science, no single factor causes autism. It would be wonderful to know the reasons so it could be prevented, but at the moment, it's suspected that a combination of factors contribute to autism. More importantly, you are not to blame. I made the mistake of blaming myself, assuming I'd done something wrong during my pregnancy. I wouldn't want anyone else to make the same mistake.

You are not responsible.

I often worried about having children. I'm aware of my defects, and I know how genetics work. What if I passed on my negative traits to my child? It bothered me a lot. It still does.

Ishanvi's diagnosis opened Pandora's box. I realized that mental illness runs on my side of the family and wondered if autism was a byproduct of that, if I was somehow responsible for passing it to her. Pravin is from an affluent family who have consistently married within their caste, a practice meant to preserve purity. By marrying me, Pravin dared to break that tradition.

I am an exception in his family, and I wondered if I had diluted his terrific gene pool. The more I thought about it, the more depressed I became. I wanted to know what could have caused Ishanvi's autism. It was only natural.

Pravin noticed I was lost in thought and asked what was bothering me. When I explained, he said, "We don't know, and it doesn't matter. Think of all the good qualities you may have passed on. Your talent, your patience, your zest for life."

"Your intelligence, quietness, and critical thinking," I added.

What started as a discussion about my insecurities became an enumeration of our good qualities. Eventually, we listed those we didn't want to pass along.

"Your laziness." I laughed.

"Your over analyzing everything," he fired back.

It was cathartic. I loved the way we listed each other's strengths and weaknesses.

We don't know which side of the family, if either, was responsible. But we can make sure we impart our best qualities to our children by being role models. Some virtues can be taught, while others are genetic. We focus on those we can control.

Autism doesn't define my little girl. She'll find herself and her purpose, eventually. For now, she's a kid, and we're letting her be. We focus on teaching our children the right things. I focus on academics and life values, while Pravin teaches them the tough stuff, practical life lessons. We each use the best of our personalities. I think it helps to show them that although Mom and Dad are different, we're bound by our love for each other and for them.

If Ishanvi is having trouble with her toys, she knows Pravin will help her. If she needs a new book to read, she'll ask me to look for one at the local library.

I think about how much more I can give her through lessons and experiences. We'll travel to show her the vastness of this world. I may have passed my genetic traits to her, but that doesn't make her something less. When my doubts try to pay me a visit, I remind myself of the second life lesson. No one is responsible. Not even me.

It's very easy to get lost trying to find out why we're facing a problem rather than focusing on the problem itself. Whenever a friend comes to me with a problem, I ask, "What can I do to help?"

Sometimes we need to figure out why it happened, but in the case of my daughter, I try not to blame anyone. I've become solution driven. Sometimes it's okay to let go and focus on what's in front of you. The moment we start looking for a solution, we're a step closer to finding one.

Lesson 3: Acceptance Is the Key.

When we received a diagnosis of autism, we were hesitant to share the news with family and even wondered if we should tell them. We were struggling with the news and felt ill- equipped to help others understand. Although both our families had been extremely supportive, we weren't sure they'd be able to accept the diagnosis living thousands of miles away.

They couldn't.

My mother refused to believe the diagnosis. She couldn't understand how a child who knew the alphabet and numbers and could recite twenty rhymes from memory could be deficient in anything.

Therein lies the problem. Most people have little to no experience with autistic kids, so they don't understand that it is, after all, a spectrum. These kids are not deficient, but they process the world differently. Their brains function differently. I've often noticed that kids on the spectrum are blessed with strengths their peers may not have.

Ishanvi has a very good memory. She's a quick learner. So, we overlooked the red flags. We associated her social anxiety with shyness. It's an easy mistake to make, but it was a mistake.

As the days passed, it became difficult to repeat the same conversations with my mom. I gave up. She hadn't seen Ishanvi in two years. She didn't really know her. I accepted that and moved on.

Why is it so hard to accept that your child/grandchild has special needs?

You think you got unlucky, or made mistakes, or that the higher power is punishing you for something. Those are ways of coming to terms with it, but your child is on the spectrum, no matter the reason why.

Once that acceptance sets in, you begin to look for support. That's when you start helping your child. The sooner you begin that journey, the better it is for your family.

Once you make peace with your child's diagnosis, you no longer experience shame. It's just the way your life has turned out. You accept it and are ready to face whatever challenges lie ahead.

Pravin accepted it before I did. He's a more practical person. I carried Ishanvi for nine months and fed her from my body for two years, so I felt more responsible.

A few decades back, mothers who didn't connect with the child were suspected of causing autism. When I read that, my heart sank, but I realized how lucky I was to be living at a time when that theory had been debunked. I can't imagine the trauma that idea must have caused mothers with autistic children.

When you don't accept your child's diagnosis, you experience another kind of trauma. You become mired in negativity and can't move on. And the innocent child suffers most.

Acceptance takes time. Do whatever you need to, but learn to accept the diagnosis. Your child needs it more than you do.

So much of life is beyond our control, and learning to accept an uncomfortable truth helps us find perspective. I believe the journey is the same with loss or grief. We can't control who leaves us or when, and the process of coping begins with acceptance.

I recently spoke to a friend who had lost her little girl in an accident. She told me that the moment she accepted that her child was gone, she came back to reality.

For a long time, I didn't want to share Ishanvi's diagnosis. When I overheard Pravin sharing it with a common friend, I became very angry. I hadn't yet accepted that truth. Sharing it made it real.

The journey becomes smoother once you find acceptance and move on.

Reintroducing Ishanvi to Family

For two years following the diagnosis, we didn't see our families. It wasn't intentional, but it was helpful. Although we'd received our Green Card, COVID-19 meant it was unsafe to travel internationally. I don't know if I would have been ready to meet them before that. Although I needed their support, I also needed to process the diagnosis on my own.

I was nervous. My family had finally accepted Ishanvi's autism but hadn't seen her since the diagnosis. I didn't know how they would react. Pravin had the same thoughts about his side of the family. But on a cool, crisp afternoon in December 2022 when we landed in New Delhi, my worries flew away.

I believe everyone came with their own pre-conceived notions. Would seeing them make the little girl anxious? Would she have a tantrum? Would she even recognize them?

When they saw how innocent and cheerful she was, their hearts melted. I saw the watchful look on my stubborn mother's face as she watched her play. I saw my father feed her fish with his own hands, periodically looking at me for direction or validation. He'd been with me in Kathmandu when Ishanvi had her meltdown, which had left a huge impact.

They were all worried. It was visible. But they adjusted. You don't want your family to remind you that your child is different. Life gives you enough reminders.

You also don't want to hear, "Your child looks normal."

I get that a lot. Ishanvi doesn't have a physical deformity and so long as she behaves typically, it's hard to tell she's autistic. But that doesn't mean she isn't. As her mother, I know her struggles and worries. People who tell you your child looks "normal" knowing that she has autism, play with your emotions. We all hope for normal children—for the version of "normal" we've been taught to accept. But parents love their children no matter what and want them to be treated with love and respect.

My family and Pravin's gave us that. I have huge respect for them. They gave Ishanvi love and acceptance, and by extension, they gave that to Pravin and me. I don't know what they went through inside, but on the outside, they made me believe they saw a normal child, and that was enough.

There is no greater joy than seeing your child accepted and loved for who she is.

Ishanvi had a wonderful trip to India. We took her to Kaziranga National Park in Assam where she interacted with elephants and saw rhinos in their natural habitat. My brother Bibhuti, who is a Park Ranger for the state, made sure she got to interact with as many animals as possible. Those gestures from family members warmed my heart.

There were challenges, too. She hated the texture of the sheets on her bed, so we put her familiar blanket over them. When it was time to return to my parents' house in Guwahati, she didn't want to leave the hotel in Kaziranga and cried for fifteen minutes while everyone looked at me for a solution.

I took my mother to my room, gave her the stuffed elephant I'd bought for one of my nieces, and asked her to give it to Ishanvi. It would be a prize for returning to Grandma's house where we'd stay until we flew back to the States. She understood and started playing with the elephant. Everyone sighed with relief. They'd gotten a taste of my life. We never know what's going to upset her, but we take a deep breath and look for a solution. We try to live.

The Nepal leg of our trip was cancelled because of rising cases of COVID in Kathmandu. So, we had time to kill, and we used it to give her more experiences. We traveled to Haridwar in Northern India and showed her the holy river Ganges. She remained calm and composed throughout the trip and we were so proud.

THE GIRL WHO FLAPS HER HANDS

By the end of that trip, I was overwhelmed with gratitude. Our families, though orthodox, accepted her as she was. During the two years since her diagnosis, I might have discussed autism with them occasionally. They are with me in learning lesson number three, the need for acceptance, which is a huge blessing.

Lesson 4: Focus on Support

Once you accept the diagnosis, it's time to put your strategies to work. You're the child's parent, so you know your child better than anyone. Doctors can only observe and recommend. They collect most of their data through parent interviews, so you play a crucial role.

Along with the diagnosis, the doctors will give you a plan with resources and options, which will likely include existing therapies and interventions. I was given so much information, it took time to process.

I started doing my own research and found that the most talked about therapy for autism, Applied Behavior Analysis, is controversial. Although I was looking for hope, I found stories of abuse and mistreatment, and that scared me. I needed more time.

Then the pandemic hit.

We had just moved and were about to restart our life in a town where we had access to the best services. But everything was shut down. While the whole world was about the pandemic, I was lost in my own struggles. Bivan's health complications at birth made him especially susceptible to COVID-19.

It had taken us a long time to partially potty train Ishanvi. She still needed a diaper when she had to poop, but at least she was peeing in the potty. When we moved to Naperville, the new apartment gave her so much anxiety, she went back to diapers full time.

It was tough, and dealing with postpartum depression made it tougher.

But we never stopped looking for help.

We continued to read about ABA, Applied Behavior Analysis. We joined an online group for families with special needs. The more you connect with people who are going through or have been through the same experience, the more normal life feels, and you know you're not alone.

I read stories about kids who'd had successful lives despite the difficulties, like Dr. Temple Gardin, an autistic pioneering scientist, who, like Ishanvi, loves animals. Those stories gave me hope.

It was chaos, but we learned to adapt and adjust our expectations.

Finally, after months of research and waiting, we found a reputable therapy center in Chicagoland. Pravin and I held each other's hands and said, "Let's go for it."

Our insurance approved forty hours of therapy a week, but we were hesitant to send her for that long. So, we started with twenty hours. We promised each other that if either of us felt she was suffering, we'd pull her out immediately. We were willing to take the help but prepared to let it go if we felt the fit wasn't right.

I connected with a number of families who shared their experience with ABA. Not all their stories had positive endings. I understood. Not every child is the same. But I appreciated their willingness to share.

Devin Cassidy, a Board-Certified Behavior Analyst, evaluated Ishanvi. She set goals for her and gave us regular updates on the programs she ran. Initially, the goals were mostly speech related. Ishanvi used about twenty words, but no sentences, and her speech was unclear.

Within six months of ABA therapy, we saw progress. She began interacting with us. My little girl was finally talking to me. I was overjoyed.

July 2022 marks two years of her ABA journey. So far, she's doing well. She still has irrational fear and anxiety. But I discuss that with Devin, and we figure out ways to tackle it. People often ask if the driving is overwhelming. Ishanvi's therapy center is twenty-two miles from our home. But we make trips to her therapy center little family outings.

For the first year in the middle of COVID, Pravin drove her three times a week while I stayed home with Bivan. Every Friday, all three of us picked her up, and on the way back, we picked up food. Ishanvi had started talking a little, and I loved how chirpy she usually was, talking about her sessions. I wanted to hear her talk, even a little.

We didn't have much trouble driving our daughter fifty miles a day, because the therapy services were excellent. Devin Cassidy changed our lives. She has been instrumental in understanding Ishanvi and making her learn. She understands my daughter almost as well as I do. Whenever she hit a roadblock, Devin figured out a plan to get around it.

When Ishanvi developed her fear of ceiling fans, Devin talked to her about her feelings and devised a mindfulness practice to help her stay calm. Devin no longer is her therapist, but the team we work with now keeps Ishanvi on track.

My fighting spirit came to life through these interactions. I knew there would always be problems or obstacles, and that we had to be willing to fight them. My child deserves that.

If ABA had not worked for us, like a lot of families, we would have looked for alternatives to help with her speech and behavior.

If you still haven't found a plan for your child, keep looking, keep experimenting. Know when to stop, but don't stop looking. Some parents decide they only want to treat a few specific symptoms, such as speech and occupational therapy. I believe that's okay, too. We're all doing our best and I respect that.

Once the kids start school, there will be more support. Kids with Ishanvi's diagnosis have the right to an Individualized Education Plan (IEP). Under Federal law, this is a legal document, which is developed for each child with special needs who attends public school in the US. The school and parents work together to devise a plan.

When we had our first IEP meeting in Iowa, we felt like the dumbest people in the room. The team used words we'd never heard before, describing techniques, methods and services. Clearly, we weren't prepared. I came home that day feeling like an inadequate mother. Then I went back to my research.

By the time her next annual IEP meeting came up, I was more equipped emotionally and intellectually. A lot of us will take similar paths, especially those who are new to the US system. That's okay. We all learn and evolve.

Today, we are in constant communication with our IEP team to make sure she gets the support she needs. My relatives in India often compliment me for taking care of my kids without help. But I remind them I'm not doing it alone. I have wonderful therapists, teachers, and school staff, and I'm grateful for them every single day. My village is populated with teachers who have understood Ishanvi and me and offered to help her.

We make sure those wonderful souls know how grateful we are. We send holiday cards and give them something special during Teacher Appreciation Week. I've bought books for my kids, and I ask every person who has worked with them—therapists, teachers, case managers—to write a personal message when their work is finished.

When Ishanvi and Bivan graduate high school, I'll present them with these books. I want them to always remember those who helped them realize their potential. They need to know we didn't do it alone. Being grateful is a wonderful virtue, and this is my way of teaching that to my children.

I don't expect my kids to be like the people I've read about whose autism hasn't prevented them from becoming successful. I don't expect my kids to be like them, but their stories give me hope. I often interact with families with special needs kids, and I try to spread awareness through my work in the community. Through a support group I run for moms with special needs kids, I've made wonderful connections. Our struggles, though our own, are similar to those other moms experience and knowing that is liberating. We understand each other better in a lot of ways. We learn from others' experiences but have the freedom to make our own decisions.

I've learned that I alone have the power to change my destiny. I know now that I'm not alone on this journey, and I've come to realize that I need to focus on support for Ishanvi and to help others find that support in order to build a community. Finding support for any issue is an important step toward solving it. If we think our kids can benefit from extra help through a form of therapy or a social skills group, we should be more than willing to offer them that.

By finding ways to support your beautiful child, you keep hope alive.

For quite some time, I felt alone in this journey. I was an immigrant without family in the States. Who could I ask for help?

The moment we were stable, with Ishanvi's therapies and our life in general, I realized it was time to reach out to others who needed help. I didn't want anyone else to go through this alone. So, Pravin and I connected with families who were either expecting a diagnosis of autism or had just received one.

We reached out to families all over the US, and after my visit to India, some families there, as well. I wanted others to know that they weren't alone.

We were immensely rewarded for our efforts. We formed connections we hadn't known were possible. I've been able to make friends with other special needs parents through a small support group I organized in my town. This has helped Ishanvi make new friends. Atypical kids seem to understand each other well. Ishanvi needs frequent breaks during playtime and almost all her atypical friends understand that, which means she's free from the pressure of trying to behave in a certain way. Sometimes she wants to flap her hands to show happiness or excitement, and her friends accept that. I want her to have connections with other kids who allow her to be herself. I'm so grateful that I've been able to generate those opportunities for her.

A lot of people compliment us for helping other families cope. I don't see it that way. It's my way of giving back to the universe. I didn't have anyone to support me, so I want to make sure that any family who needs support gets it.

I hope that when my kids see us giving our time to those families, they'll learn that they can do it, too. Helping people is a way of living a good life. It uplifts the community and brings about positive change. I want my kids to choose that before anything else.

For example, let's consider birthday parties. Ishanvi's idea of a birthday party is balloons and attention, and she doesn't like that.

When she turned five, I tried to organize a birthday party for her, and our friends made a big fuss about it. As we were preparing, Ishanvi went missing in action. I found her in her bed upstairs under the blanket.

She said she felt uneasy.

I should have guessed. She was overwhelmed. We realized it was a mistake, but we already had guests in the house, so we went on with the party. I didn't force her to join us, but eventually, she came down on her own, cut her cake and proceeded to play with her friends. After that, we stopped planning birthday parties for her.

The first time I took her to another kid's birthday party, she didn't last fifteen minutes. There was a balloon artist and every time a friend showed her a balloon, she freaked out.

Birthday parties may not be part of our family tradition, but we've come to terms with that. For a while, though, it seemed unfair not to be able to enjoy something as simple as a birthday party.

In the fall of 2022, realizing that Ishanvi loves Halloween, I invited her closest friends to a party at our house and treated it like a birthday party. The focus was not on her but on Halloween. I thought it would be an opportunity to reciprocate for all the wonderful birthdays we'd been invited to. At the same time, I could support Ishanvi, letting her have her day.

Before the guests arrived, I showed her the decorations, and even tried to place some balloons. She was playing happily with my friend Deborah when one of the balloons popped. She screamed and went upstairs. It was time for damage control.

I explained that balloons pop and that makes a sound. I said if they made her uncomfortable, we'd take them away so she could enjoy the party. She came downstairs to be sure I was telling the truth. Then she seemed to forget all about the balloons and had fun, especially when Princess Snow White arrived to entertain the kids. It worked like magic, and we host an amazing Halloween party for her every year.

There it was, hope that my daughter would finally enjoy a party. It may not be traditional, but I don't care. I'm figuring out how to make her childhood as memorable as possible. She may not have a birthday party, but she has a Halloween party, and that's our family's normal.

Lesson four supports come in different forms. Remember that we need to look for support not just for the kids, but for ourselves. Often, when I talk with parents of special needs kids, I sense that they feel overwhelmed. They need some sort of support, but it's nowhere to be found.

I once spoke with a mom who told me about her difficulties managing her child's issues. I asked her how she was coping. My question surprised her. She said she didn't want to bother me with her worries but wanted to discuss her child.

As parents of kids who need our constant attention, it's important to turn our attention to ourselves, as well. I asked her, "How do you plan to take care of your child when you're not feeling one hundred percent?"

Having a community of people who understand you and are willing to support you is important. We need to be prepared to work for that and to choose the right kind of support for the entire family. I'm trying my best, and I know that sometimes it's all I can do.

Through our work in the community, we connected with families, both neurotypical and special needs. Because we discuss our struggle with them, they understand.

We once planned to celebrate the birthday of a friend who cancelled at the last minute. Ishanvi had the toughest time letting that go. We couldn't barge into someone's house because our daughter couldn't understand that plans change.

I realize I could have handled it better. We were successful in diverting her attention, but I wish I could have told my friend it was rude to cancel at the last minute. They knew nothing of our struggle. We hadn't told them that Ishanvi was on the spectrum, so they had no way of knowing that a sudden change of plans would cause so much stress in our family.

Ishanvi needed to be flexible, which is always hard for kids on the spectrum. I understand that but the situation was nobody's fault.

Today, I make sure I tell my friends about the behaviors to expect from Ishanvi so we're all aware. That understanding is a type of support.

By accumulating sources of support, we make our kids' lives easier.

Lesson 5: Highlight the Strengths

Receiving a diagnosis of autism can be overpowering. We see our deficiencies on that piece of paper. When I meet a family with a kid on the spectrum, I always ask, "What is your child's strength?"

Almost always, the families react with confusion. It is not a question that they are familiar with.

I know that these kids have strengths. We just need to look.

Ishanvi is a super smart girl. She has a sharp memory. She loves animals. She's energetic, and she's willing to work on her issues. Above all, she loves to impress people. I count those all as strengths and use them to teach her valuable lessons.

When I'm filling out a form or talking about her to someone, I mention her strengths first.

In the fall of 2021 she was about to begin kindergarten, which is a full-day program in our district. It was giving me tremendous anxiety, so before school started, I decided to email her principal, Mrs. Rodriguez, introducing our family. I opened by telling her about Ishanvi's strengths. She called me right away and told me what a wonderful approach that was, and that she would use it in the future for all the children. I'd like to have that same sort of conversation with everyone I talk to about Ishanvi, and I hope that parents around the world will do that for their kids.

There was a time when I was overwhelmed by the number of forms I had to fill out—questionnaires about her behavior, forms for school, therapy centers, extra-curricular activities, and park district programs. I realize that all that information paves the way for a better future for her, because the more I share, the better her providers will be able to assist her. For parents who are new to this, remember that although it may be overwhelming, in our world, it's a necessary evil.

Your child may have anxiety and fear, but she's still a child, innocent, energetic, and full of love. You must accept that first before you present her to a world that can be intimidating, confusing and, at times, dangerous.

Based on her strengths, I started making short-term goals for Ishanvi. With so much going on, I didn't want to overwhelm her. She was already involved in an Individualized Education Plan at school, a learning plan at the ABA center, and private speech services. She is, after all, a kid who needs a normal childhood, whatever that means in today's world. After some time, we decided to omit speech services. It didn't feel necessary since her ABA goals were also speech related.

As her speech improved, I focused on the activities that really interested her. She loves animals, and she loves to travel. Every weekend, we planned fun activities with her. I bought books with animal stories and designed her room in our new home with an animal theme. I designed a playroom filled with her favorite games. I did whatever I could to keep her happy, and it worked. She has learned so much. She reads on her own and knows every little fact about the animals she loves. She takes long hikes with us and loves nature. There's a twinkle in her eyes every time I take her to a zoo or animal center.

With everything going on, it's very easy to overlook her progress, and it's important to manage expectations. How much time should we wait before seeing real results? It took six months of ABA therapy for Ishanvi to become fully verbal. She's still shy, but she can request items or tell me about her feelings. Six months ago, those were my goals for her. I waited six months for her to achieve those goals, and at times, it was agonizing.

"At the end of the day, what matters is she is trying, and we're trying with her and for her. Give yourself a pat on the back for doing as much as you are. Raising a special needs child is a constant struggle and not everyone will appreciate that. Your appreciation for yourself matters the most.

Laugh at the silly things they do, the way they interact, the silly pronunciations. I know I did. And now that my daughter is verbal, I look

back at those moments and I get so much clarity. After all, everything happens for your own good.
Stay positive, and you'll get through this."

A Positive Change

Almost six months after my conversation with the school principal, I attended my daughter's IEP meeting. The team started with a slide dedicated to her strengths. I was told that throughout the school, every child was introduced by their strengths. I'm not sure if that was a direct result of our conversation, but whatever the reason, it was something I wanted for my daughter and others like her.

Everything I do is geared toward bringing awareness of how we treat our kids and the kind of world we plan to leave for them. For me, that world absolutely must contain KINDNESS. And that can only happen if we start noticing each other's strengths, rather than focusing on the weaknesses.

Soon after, I started my blog because a lot of people in my community encouraged me to do so. And the stories I posted on social media about positive interactions with people in my community began to attract positive attention. I got messages from total strangers telling me how much my story inspired them. Some of them even asked if I wrote. I did write, but I didn't have a medium dedicated to it.

Pravin helped me put up the blog. I channeled all my good energy and started blogging. I wanted to tell people that being kind and generous matters, and I could feel that my stories were making an impact. If anyone ever tells you that you're too inconsequential to bring about change, don't you dare listen to them. Set your heart on doing something good, and you'll succeed. It might take time but keep up your resilience and determination.

We're responsible for building a better, kinder world for our kids.

I use patience and research to find solutions to the issues we face. Pravin uses his understanding of life to teach our children independence.

In July 2022, we drove a hundred miles from our vacation rental in Estes Park, Colorado to Lake Agnes in State Forest State Park. I'd added hiking the lake to our itinerary at the last minute. We'd seen all the animals we could in the Rocky Mountains except moose, and I hoped we could spot some in that part of Colorado.

By the time we reached the starting point of the hike, clouds were gathering. In the mountains, especially above the tree line, thunderstorms can be life threatening. We had a dilemma. Should we go on or head back?

Another family was gearing up for the hike, and the elderly man smiled at me, as though telling me it would be okay. So, I did something totally unlike me. I told Pravin we should go for it. He was surprised because he thought I'd need convincing. He's the risk taker in the relationship, not me.

I said a prayer, and as we started our two-mile hike, the beautiful snow-clad mountain staring at us. Although the trail was covered in snow, wildflowers were blooming. I thought of our two beautiful kids who follow us around, looking for direction. I decide which direction I want them to take, at least for now. That afternoon in Colorado, they didn't know we might be in danger. I knew, but I trusted my gut and decided to hike anyway. Was it worth it?

Hell, yes!

After about forty-five minutes, we reached pristine Lake Agnes. The water was crystal clear, perfectly mirroring the mountain. We sat quietly with our fellow hikers.

The kids played, throwing rocks into the lake while Pravin and I watched, enjoying the moment. I love these moments of clarity when I pause and my whole life seems to be going in the right direction. This is my life, my family, and I'm living it right now. It became clear to me that although my strength is knowing and researching, sometimes it's okay to venture out of my comfort zone.

Strength, although a part of us, doesn't necessarily have to restrict us.

While it's important to be aware of our weaknesses, our strengths make us shine. I try to notice that when I interact with people. Everyone is good at something. I learned that from my boss in India. Mr. Bhattacharya is a dedicated, hardworking, passionate employee who taught me to recognize people's strengths and utilize them for the betterment of the company. I extend that to other areas of life now. Sometimes all we're looking for is someone to notice our strengths. It's a small gesture that can mean a lot.

Lesson 6: Be Kind

I was a nice person, but never a kind one.

Early in my experience of handling a special needs child, I understood why kindness is so important. I was raised to be competitive. Exams, extracurricular activities—everything was a competition. Perhaps because I grew up in one of the most populated countries in the world, I needed to fight to excel. When Ishanvi was born, I was expected to raise her in the same way, and I did.

Until the diagnosis.

When I watched her struggle through basic daily activities, my heart ached. She had trouble following instructions to wash her hands. Her day care teacher broke down the steps visually, but she still got stuck. One day, her teacher, the lovely Ms. Amy, told me that a little girl, who was a year younger than Ishanvi, had held her hand while she washed. When asked what made her do that, she said she saw Ishanvi getting stuck and wanted to help. I teared up. It was pure kindness, something I want every day for my daughter.

For a long time, Ishanvi was afraid to go down the slide at the playground. She'd climb the steps but froze when she reached the top. A little girl waiting behind her became agitated and tried to bully her. I saw that Ishanvi was nervous and caught the girl pretending to hit her. Ishanvi screamed and ran to me. On the ride home, I had a small awakening. I decided that instead of being angry at that little girl, I'd change. I made amends to everyone I thought I'd hurt. There weren't many, but it was a small step toward a bigger goal. I had to change myself so I could ask others to change their behavior toward my child. Not everyone would, but I had to try.

It was no less than cathartic. I was liberated emotionally and mentally. Subsequently, I began preaching kindness in all the forums I participated in. I advised other mothers to inculcate kindness in their children. My goal was to inspire the behavior I wanted my child to embody and receive. You cannot change the world, but you can start somewhere. It's my way of hoping Ishanvi will be treated with kindness wherever she goes.

As I began to interact with parents and caregivers of special needs children, I was amazed and disheartened to hear stories of discrimination and negligence. I can only hope the world will change its attitude toward these children. As a parent, I do my best to spread that message. My goal is to get rid of the stigma. You should be able to introduce your special needs child as proudly as you would if he were neurotypical, without thinking about judgement, prejudice, or preconceived notions. You should be proud of the child you birthed.

I advise parents to mention why they need kindness. In my opinion, that's true learning. Lesson six changed my perspective on life. I now realize that we are responsible for the tiny humans in our care.

"Every little act of kindness counts. Please make your children believe that. Kindness can change the world, more so for a special needs child.

The Special Llama

"Kindness in words creates confidence. Kindness in thinking creates profoundness. Kindness in giving creates love."
— Lao Tzu

In 2020 after we received our Green Card, we decided to invest in our first house. We'd decided to settle down in the US because of the support Ishanvi had there. By Thanksgiving, we'd moved to our new house, but there was pressure to fit in, and I was confused about holiday protocol in the neighborhood.

Celebrating the holidays in the US was a new concept to me, and I embraced it as much as I could. I'd been told to compare this time of the year with the Indian festival Diwali, which we celebrate by exchanging gifts with near and dear ones. We also reward the people whose services help make our lives easier and better.

In that spirit, I planned to gift something nice to my daughter's school bus driver, Mel. Ishanvi had started formal school that academic year. It had been a journey of learning for me, too, as I tried to adjust to the American way of living. Mel was a lovely young woman who always greeted us with a bright smile. So, on the Friday before Christmas break, I waited for the bus with a gift bag, beaming with pride, secretly patting myself on the back for having adjusted to American culture so quickly.

To my surprise, when I got on the bus, Mel was ready with a gift bag for my daughter. I accepted it with a smile but was a bit taken aback. I didn't know what to do. My aim was to make Mel's day brighter by offering a gift. Instead, there I was, perplexed, trying to buckle up Ishanvi. Mel broke the silence and asked me to open the gift. She was sure Ishanvi would love it.

As soon as my daughter opened it, her face lit up with joy. It was her favorite stuffed animal, a llama.

Mel explained that she'd gone to several stores trying to find a purple llama. I must have told her in passing that purple is Ishanvi's favorite color. She'd listened. She also must have noticed that my daughter carries a lot of llama stuff with her.

I got off the bus, trying to contain the thousands of emotions going through my heart. As parents, you want nothing but the best for your child. The biggest struggle is letting the kids spend the entire day in the care of people unknown to you at some level. When those people are like Mel, your worry vanishes. That was the biggest gift she could have given me that holiday season.

The joy she brought to my little girl by paying attention to what she might like, even making an extra effort, touched my heart. School is a short drive from our home, so Mel only spent five minutes a day with Ishanvi, but that was enough for her to know the kid she was driving to school and make her happy.

I noticed that Mel had several other gift bags with her. It wasn't hard to guess that a lot of kids were surprised that day.

As I stood in my driveway watching the bus leave and waving goodbye to Ishanvi, the holiday spirit finally hit me. Mel showed me what it is to truly care for someone without expecting anything in return. To show kindness and compassion. Ishanvi will never forget that gesture, and neither will I. She carries her "special llama" with her everywhere she goes.

In January 2022, when we came back from our trip to India, Mel was there to welcome Ishanvi at the bus stop first thing in the morning. She'd decorated Ishanvi's side of the seat and the window with llama stickers and given her llama-themed activity sheets, just in time for Valentine's Day. Ishanvi's joy knew no bounds. Mel had done her magic again. The magic of spreading much needed love.

I published this story on my blog and shared it with her IEP Team in one of the meetings when the question of transportation came up. We live pretty close to the school, but I'd insisted on the school bus because I thought of it as a positive reinforcement for Ishanvi. One day, I got a call from her school principal, the lovely Mrs. Rodriguez, wanting my permission to share this story with the Head of Transportation, Mel's boss. I was happy to. Mel deserves every bit of praise, and I was glad to be part of it.

"Never doubt that a small group of thoughtful, committed citizens can change the world; indeed, it's the only thing that ever has."
— Margaret Mead

When Ishanvi was bullied at summer camp, two friends stood beside her. I was told they had her back. She has made friends at school who play with her, and don't see her differently. You have to admit, as a kid, if you're playing with a kid who starts flapping her hands without any warning, it's natural to get curious. I've been in the middle of those situations. I look at Ishanvi and her friend visibly confused. I step in and say, "Ishanvi is extremely happy to play with you and that's how she shows her happiness, by flapping her hands." I want the friend to know that flapping is okay. It's acceptable and not something questionable. That's the world I want to live in, where Ishanvi's flapping is considered "normal."

On every step of my journey, I've met kind and caring people who helped build my faith. The world is full of these beautiful souls, and I hope Ishanvi encounters them throughout her life's journey.

Lesson 7: Embrace Your Child's Individuality

When I was ready to talk openly about Ishanvi's diagnosis, I realized how liberating it was. I no longer restricted myself to meeting only special needs parents. I believe that while our role as parents of these beautiful children is important, so is the role of parents of neurotypical children. Some may disagree. I have met these people.

Ishanvi's world will not be restricted to children like her. She'll meet kids who are oblivious to her diagnosis and parents who have no idea how to approach her. Her best friend may be a neurotypical child who will have to deal with her quirks. Isn't it a good idea to make every family aware of special kids like Ishanvi? To let them know that we expect them to give our kids a chance? These kids need to coexist.

I realized that I needed to be careful in my approach. I didn't share her diagnosis with random people, but took my time, observed them, and when I knew the time was right, I told them.

Most people took it well. Some asked how I managed. Some told me God would compensate for what she lacks through another child. Some said they hadn't realized she had special needs. Some made it a mission to make their own child aware and to be more kind. Some backed away.

Different people, different reactions. The way I phrased my message was important: she's different, she's a child, she deserves a chance, and so do all the kids like her.

"I never wanted autism to define my little girl. She is so much more than that. She is kind, funny, smart, and beautiful. All these adjectives are what make her the person she is: HER OWN PERSON."

I think most of the stigma and embarrassment comes from the concept of parenting and giving birth. We expect our children to be unique—and they are, each in their OWN way, which may not be our way. Our idea of uniqueness needs to change.

We all need to accept that—including the parents of neurotypical kids. We need to stop expecting too much from our kids, or ask them to carry our batons, or be the person we couldn't be. We need to allow them to breathe and follow their own paths so they can realize their purposes sooner than later. Trust me, you'll be doing them a huge favor.

Over the years, I've come to realize that the more I expect my daughter to behave in a certain way, the more disappointment I suffer. So long as she's not hurting anyone physically, I let her be. She has her quirks. At first, when she was quirky in public, we were embarrassed. We now know that having her has made us happier, because she does so many things that make us laugh.

Her repetition of words, funny reactions, random dances, quiet sobbing, and unexpected hugs are little blessings in our lives. We wouldn't want to change anything. The only worry we have is whether the rest of the world will be able to appreciate her. That's why I want to spread awareness as much as I can.

Every person is unique, and we must embrace that with our whole hearts. Lesson six liberated me in ways I couldn't have imagined. I love my daughter just the way she is. I also believe she's meant to bring about a greater change in this world. She's innocent and kind, and I want her to keep those virtues as long as possible.

An Appeal for Compassion

"*It is not our job to toughen our children up to face a cruel and heartless world. It's our job to raise children who will make the world a little less cruel and heartless.*"

\- L. R. Knost, founder of Little Hearts/Gentle Parenting Resources

In the fall of 2021, I was a nervous wreck. Ishanvi was about to start full days at school. I knew I was right to be concerned about her, that comes with the territory. But I began wondering what I could do to make it better for her, to ensure that her peers would be kind to her. I concluded it was my duty to reach out, to ask mothers to please let their kids know they'd meet all kinds of friends at school—and in life:

- friends who may not look like them
-friends who may not be able to talk
-friends who may need help walking
-friends who may be shy
- friends who may talk a lot

I hope they tell their kids that every child they meet is worth getting to know better. Every child is worth their love, and those who seem the most difficult may need their love the most.

I spend a lot of time with parents like me who are blessed with a special needs child. I understand them, their struggles, their pain, their joy. As much as I love spending time with them and listening to their stories, I feel it's just as important to reach out to parents who are blessed with neurotypical kids, many of whom may not know how to respond to parents like me.

"I'm a strong advocate of inclusiveness. I believe society can flourish only if we know each other's pain and joy."

How can I expect others to be kind to my daughter if they don't know the challenges she was born with? How can anyone be truly empathetic without knowing the situation that demands it?

THE GIRL WHO FLAPS HER HANDS

I always ask my community—the strong mothers, the overwhelmed mothers, the working mothers, the stay-at-home mothers, the mothers of a special needs child, the teachers, doctors, coaches and hairdressers—to please advocate kindness to their kids and to be kind themselves, to teach kindness as they would teach independence. It's important that kids learn both.

Our children are the future of this beautiful world, and we need them to be kind. That way, we know we're leaving them in a kinder world and that they'll be safe without us, be it in school or in life.

This thought became my first foray into publishing in the US. Since then, I've written about my experiences with kindness numerous times. I've visited colleges and had pivotal conversations with students. I've created support groups where kindness and acceptance of others are discussed. I think embracing uniqueness and being kind are intertwined. It's important to realize that some kids are different and should be treated with kindness.

"Please teach your kids to be kind, to be compassionate.
One act of kindness can change the whole world. It can change someone's
perspective—their day—even their life."

Lesson 8: Find Your Inner Joy

The year following the diagnosis was the hardest to navigate. We were dealing with so much—our big move, our visa situation, another baby to care for. But we got through it all.

One day, I gave up on God. It wasn't sudden. The anger had been building for quite some time. I was brought up in a household where I enjoyed religious freedom. But the pandemic, combined with Ishanvi's struggle, brought out the worst in me. Eventually, I decided to take God out of the equation. I wasn't worried. I was up for a challenge. Even if God existed, what could he do? I had nothing to lose.

I survived for a year and a half without God in my life. I didn't try to bring him back. I no longer cared. These are the journeys we go through, as parents of neurodivergent kids, journeys of trust and failure.

I threw away all the God-related stuff in my house. I was done. I was struggling and thought God wasn't doing his part. He was supposed to care for me when I was in need. So, to avoid any more disappointment, I let God go. I needed to stop expecting things to change for the better.

When we bought our new home, I performed none of the customary religious rituals. I didn't even have the traditional Hindu temple in the house. I needed time before I could trust again.

I realize now that a lot of people lose or question their faith when they feel overwhelmed or sad or when they're forced to believe there's no light at the end of the tunnel. We all do what we must to cope with life. And life is hard, there's no denying it.

Eventually, I made my peace with God. I'm back to trusting Him, and I love that I took my own sweet time. I had to. It was my journey, after all. All the while, Pravin didn't say a word. I respect him for that. I wasn't sure if my behavior had made him a non-believer, as well. We never talked about it. We didn't need to. He was with me when I threw my faith away. And he was with me almost a year later when we bought a small temple for our new home. Sometimes I wonder if I deserve him. Long ago, he promised to stand by me till his last breath, no matter what. And he has kept that promise.

After an intense year, we decided to shift focus and give Ishanvi some room. She'd started making progress, and we wanted to cherish that. I also realized how important it was to support my partner. We were both overwhelmed, and we needed to lift each other up. We tried.

We got talking and realized that we hadn't been on a date in over a year and a half. Socializing seemed trivial in the midst of Ishanvi's therapies. It had been all about her. It was time for us to distribute our attention wisely. And we had another child to care for.

We started small. For some time, I'd wanted to leave Ishanvi at home with a sitter—not any sitter, but someone who had experience with special needs kids. I did some research and found a special education teacher in the district who was willing to take the job for a few hours each week. It made a tremendous difference. We celebrated our anniversary at a restaurant. It was a small step toward a life that needed attention, our shared life as partners.

I advise other parents to take care of their relationships. Although parenting is a 24/7 job, it's okay to take a break. These kids and their needs consume our time, but we can't forget that we're individuals with our own dreams. We need to nourish ourselves, as well.

Meeting people and sharing your stories will broaden your mind. Don't let the diagnosis take over everything you've built up. It is an important part, but not the entirety of your existence.

Follow your hobbies, go out with friends, make new connections, and enjoy life.

I used to think enjoyment was overrated. It's subjective. Some find happiness in the pages of a book, while others find it in a noisy club. Regardless, finding what brings you joy and cherishing it is crucial. We each get one life, and difficulties will come and go, but memories remain. It up to us to create good ones.

One day while Ishanvi was playing in the kitchen, she spilled milk all over the floor. I was furious, but she said, "It's okay to spill milk."

The night before, I'd read her the book *Be Who You Are* by Todd Parr. She was experimenting to see if the book applied to real life. My anger flew away, and I realized it was a moment to cherish.

Kids teach us so many life lessons. It's up to us to identify those moments and cherish them forever. Life has so much more to offer than we can perceive. Every moment with your kid is special. You just need to see it. Over time, Ishanvi's quirks, which had troubled us, began making sense, and we almost liked them. It wasn't neurotypical behavior, but it was special.

I keep saying, "Normal is overrated."

I strongly believe that. Not that I have anything against "normal," but the word needs to be redefined.

The other day, I was attending to both my kids when Bivan hit me with a water bottle. I gave him an angry look, but Ishanvi was quick to say, "It's okay, Mama. It is just a bump. We can call the doctor."

It was funny and innocent. She pressed a kiss on my head and smiled at me.

She was sympathizing with me, trying to tell me everything would be okay. Life is full of such moments. We just need clarity of thought and vision to find them.

When Ishanvi sees me dress up for my dates, she praises me. She's figured out what make-up is. She's not a diva by nature (neither was I at her age) but she knowledges that it's important.

"It's crucial that kids experience a natural social environment."

Ishanvi is learning so much from her play dates when the skills she learns in therapy are put to use. I observe her and share my notes with her BCBA. We discuss them and devise a plan to work on the areas she struggles with. The idea is not to push her, but to gently guide her. Once I caught her throwing a toy at her friend. When I shared that with her therapist, she concluded that Ishanvi was overwhelmed and wanted a break. So, we came up with a plan to ask her to "take a break" when she became visibly overwhelmed. It worked. Now she does it herself. She asks me for a break when she needs one. Informed, observant parents have the power to make things easier for their little ones.

Above all, we need to show them there's an entire world out there where they'll have to make a living. These experiences teach them that. Ishanvi realizes she's not the center of attention and that Mom and Dad have lives of their own. Maybe it will encourage her to look into her core and figure out that she's an individual, too. Maybe it will guide her to her inner joy.

"A happy you will lead to a happy atmosphere at home. Kids always know when something is going on. There's no fooling them. When they see the most important person in their lives happy, they're happy, too."

For about a year after Ishanvi's diagnosis, I felt lost. It's typical, I think. I didn't know what to do with the information or how to process it. I felt judged and malnourished energy-wise. I was taking care of my son who was developing typically, but I was often lost in thought, which affected my relationships, including the one with Pravin.

I felt I didn't deserve to have fun. I was breathing but not living.

The move to Naperville didn't help. It was a new town for us, and we didn't know anyone.

Around Thanksgiving 2020, we decided it was time to settle down. We bought a house in a beautiful neighborhood in nearby Aurora, Illinois. Although it was close to Naperville, the move brought about life altering changes.

I don't know if it was because I was caring for a new house, or because Ishanvi was showing tremendous progress, but I found myself. Then on Christmas Eve, a month after we moved, while we were all sitting in the playroom, Pravin stood up, pulling Bivan by the hand. Bivan decided to sit back down, putting opposing pressure on his arm. Then he started screaming. He was fourteen months old.

I tried to put him to sleep, not realizing he was in excruciating pain. At about two in the morning, he woke up, screaming again and showing me his hand. I knew something was wrong. So, I woke up Pravin and told him I thought we should take Bivan to the Emergency Room.

We knew no one in Aurora. We didn't know where the nearest hospital was, or what to do with Ishanvi. We had no one to call for help. It was COVID time, and we weren't sure of hospital protocol.

Bivan's screams brought me back to reality. I told Pravin, "We'll see what to do when we get there."

He called his insurance company to ask about hospitals and found one about ten miles away. So, on Christmas eve when most people were gearing up for a joyful morning, we were heading to the hospital with a screaming toddler.

As expected, the hospital wouldn't allow all four of us to enter, so I volunteered to take Bivan while Pravin and Ishanvi waited in the car. Midwestern winters are brutal. Pravin had no choice but to keep the car running and the heat on while they waited for me.

It took the doctors and nurses three hours to treat his arm, which thankfully, wasn't broken. Instead, he was suffering from something called "nursemaid's elbow."

When we got home, we put the kids back to bed and sat in the living room. "We must have a community here. Today was a reminder of that," Pravin said.

I agreed.

"I am not great at making conversation, but you are. I think you should go out there and start building a community for this family."

It was so easy for him to tell me that. I've always been good at making conversation, but I'd changed a lot and no longer knew who I was. Could I go back to being my former self? Was that even possible?

I tried and I failed and tried again.

Making new friends as an adult can be tricky. I didn't have a lot of time to devote to it, but I tried my best. I believe that hard work never goes to waste when combined with good intentions.

To form a community. I had to let go of my fear of judgement. Growing up, I'd had a lot of hobbies—singing, dancing, and writing, to name a few. With every connection I made, I was able to get in touch with my younger self and my hobbies. I sang and danced and wrote like never before.

My best discovery was storytelling. I'd been sharing my stories on social media but never in front of a crowd. With my newfound confidence and the support of a local woman, I got on stage and began telling stories. More opportunities to tell stories in Chicagoland followed.

Through this process, I met fellow storytellers in the area who encouraged me to speak at various events. I felt I was able to make an impact with my stories. Today, I speak on several platforms and try to bring awareness about autism. I tell everyone who listens to my stories or reads my blog that every act of kindness and humanity matters, that these kids deserve love.

Somewhere along the line, I discovered myself. I have my faults, but I found myself, my enjoyment. A happy me surely keeps the family happy.

My friends often ask me how I manage to do so much. The credit goes to Pravin. When I told him I wanted to do storytelling, he asked what I needed from him. I told him he would have to take care of the kids while I was gone. I wanted to start a book club in my community and volunteer for newsletters, which would mean time away from the kids. He assured me that he would be there for whatever I needed to feel like myself again. I think he knew I'd been struggling to be myself for a long time and was happy I was willing to put myself out there, no matter the consequence. If that's not love, I don't know what is.

I have been a part of the storytelling community since March 2021. The Book Club, A Novel Bunch, had their first author guest, the fabulous Bonnie Garmus, author of *Lessons in Chemistry*. I have interacted with so many intelligent, smart people over the course of this journey. I was able to do this because I have Pravin's support. I cannot be myself without Pravin, that much is true. With his support, I can leave the house without worrying about our kids.

This also brings the whole discussion about gender-specific roles prevalent in our society. When my kids see their dad taking care of them, making food in the kitchen, they learn that those are not just a woman's responsibilities.

Pravin stays up late when I'm out so he can ask me how it went when I get home. Sometimes, we talk until early morning, aware that Bivan will wake us up in a few hours. Our discussions can be never ending, just like our love. A good partner will always make sure you find yourself when you need to. But you need to begin the journey yourself.

91

Lesson 9: Celebrate Victories

Victories are so important.

During the past two years, I've gone through so much as a mother. It's hard to put that into words. When I look back, I see my struggle, but I also see my victories. Our victories.

From Ishanvi's first complete sentence to finally answering the question, "What's your name?" Each victory was important and joyful. We started with small goals. Simple conversations. Answering the speech therapist's "what, where, why, when" questions. Sustained attendance at activities. Letting me know when she needs to go pee. Using a sentence so we wouldn't have to figure out what she was trying to say with body language. The first time she pooped in the potty. Verbalizing that she was hungry rather than pointing at things in the pantry. Those were all victories that deserved to be celebrated.

I always say Ishanvi is a blessing in my life. She changed me.

I was never a kind person. I often judged people, classifying things in black and white. Now I give them the benefit of the doubt. I don't take things to heart, and I've thrown away my ego.

I don't expect everyone to follow this. But I sincerely hope people will change and evolve. Our children, whether neurotypical or special needs, deserve that.

"Don't be so burdened by the struggle that you overlook the small wins."

Commemorate a speech milestone by taking a trip to your child's favorite ice cream store. Celebrate diaper-free days with her favorite meal. Whatever it is, celebrate. She'll see your joy and gain confidence. She'll know she matters.

Never criticize her publicly or try to tell her she's less than her peers.

She's unique, and she's your child. Make her feel special.

Above all, normalize joy in your family.

A family who celebrates small victories won't struggle when hardship strikes.

We celebrate Ishanvi every single day.

Her birthday week is a festival for us. We take a weeklong vacation and I plan the best things for her. We gave her the experiences of taking a flight, navigating crazy airport crowds, hiking for miles without a snack, meeting strangers, and being cordial. These life experiences will remain with her. We want her to know that a victory can be good grades or a successful hike through difficult terrain. She needs to diversify her notion of "success," and so does society.

Someday I plan to take her to meet the renowned autistic scientist Dr. Temple Grandin.

I take so much comfort in her journey from shy little girl to successful career-oriented woman. I want people to read these stories because they offer hope.

In 2021, we took her to the Smoky Mountains where we saw bears. She was overjoyed. I surprised her with a personal meetup with a penguin. She surprised me by bravely taking an unplanned rafting trip down the river. Her birthday was a hit.

I strive every day to see a smile on her face. I plan things for her and wait patiently for the giggles that make my day. They give me the satisfaction of knowing I'm doing a good job as her mother. And I celebrate them every time.

"Take this moment to bring your family together. Embrace that
quirkiness. Celebrate those family dinners, family outings.
Make traditions, break traditions, and make memories."

Because Ishanvi has worked so much on her anxiety, while we were in the Smokies, we made an impromptu decision to go tubing on the river, and she sat there like a queen. I didn't have time to prepare her because it wasn't on our schedule. But she cooperated. That made me proud. She's learning not to be affected by uncertainty.

Those are victories for me. And I'll celebrate them as long as I live.

A Tubing Surprise

In 2021, we celebrated Ishanvi's fifth birthday in the Smokey Mountains. As always, I planned the vacation in detail. She was scheduled to meet penguins at the aquarium in Gatlinburg, take an early morning drive to Cades Cove to spot animals, and have a fantastic experience at the Anakeesta theme park. The list was long.

We prefer to stay in quieter towns, especially because we travel during the week of July Fourth, when these places are crowded. We picked a beautiful, rustic cabin in Sevierville, Tennessee and used the Townsend entrance to the park.

On our way there, we noticed a lot of tubers floating on Little River. Pravin was curious. I knew what that meant. Trouble!

By the second day, he wanted to go tubing. I told him he could go, but the kids and I wouldn't accompany him. It wasn't part of my itinerary, and it seemed dangerous. But he convinced me.

So, after lunch we headed to the rental place in Townsend where we'd seen tubes gathered. There we were told that the tube would float freely downstream, and their staff would guide us at the exit point a few miles away. I was getting nervous for the kids.

Pravin said he would handle Bivan. Ishanvi and I each got our own float. Pravin suggested we tie our floats together. I didn't object.

But we didn't plan well. When Pravin put the tubes in the water, Ishanvi sat on hers before we could tie it to ours. Off she went with the river current.

I panicked for a second, then jumped onto my tube and followed her. Pravin and I locked eyes in agreement. He'd take care of Bivan while I rescued Ishanvi.

I soon caught up with her. I was worried she'd be scared, but she was so calm, it took me by surprise. I tied my tube to hers and we reached steady water.

I looked back to see where the other half of the family was. Pravin was barely holding Bivan, who wanted to jump into the water from his lap. I burst into laughter.

We united and tied the floats together. I thought the rest of the journey would go smoothly, but the ripples began getting bigger until they became fierce. Ishanvi's tube seemed unstable, so Pravin transferred Bivan to me in case he was needed to hold on to it.

Sure enough, Ishanvi toppled into the river and Pravin caught her just in time. The river wasn't very deep, and she was super tall for her age. She could have easily stood, but she felt pebbles on the riverbed under her feet and didn't like it.

That was the start of a stressful journey back to shore.

Pravin held on to her and tried to tell her to calm down, but she was adamant that she didn't want to stand. That meant he'd have to pick her up. She was heavy, but he managed to carry her toward the shore, which was lined with cottages.

Both Pravin's and Ishanvi's tubes were floating around empty, and one of them got stuck on a big rock.

I had to do something about the stuck tube. It was blocking mine, so I couldn't move.

Pravin told me to get into the water and free it, then jump back onto my tube and push it toward the shore so he and Ishanvi could hop in.

That seemed impossible. I couldn't swim, so even jumping into four-foot-deep water wasn't an option. And Bivan was asleep on my lap. I'd have to jump with him. If I had a bad landing, we'd both fall into the river. If I lost my grip, I wouldn't be able to retrieve him, and he might drown.

Pravin kept screaming because he couldn't hold Ishanvi much longer.

Finally, I took God's name and jumped, holding on to Bivan as though my life depended on it, and I made a smooth landing.

Slowly, I let go of my fear and walked to shore. Bivan was crying, unable to comprehend what was happening.

When I got close to shore, Pravin put Ishanvi on her tube and hopped on to his. We made sure we were all tied together and pushed on down the river without saying a word until we got to the exit point.

By that time, it was getting dark. We got there just as the last of the staff were about to leave.

As we were taking off our life jackets, Ishanvi gave me a big smile and said, "Mama, I'm a brave girl." With a thumbs up.

My heart melted. I looked at Pravin and his expression confirmed that we were okay now.

Ishanvi came out of that experience knowing she'd done her best. Sure, I got some grey hair during those anxious fifteen minutes alone, but as long as we're safe, I'm good. It was a victory.

We took the bus to the starting point where we'd parked our car.

"Don't ever ask me to change my itinerary again," I told Pravin.

He nodded.

PART 3
After

It's been two years since Ishanvi's diagnosis. During those two years, I've changed from a stubborn, competitive woman to a kind, caring human being. I never knew kindness the way I do now. I realize how important it is for us, especially our kids, and I've forgiven people whom I felt did wrong by me.

I'm mending bridges

I'm rebuilding relationships.

Perhaps it was my fate to give birth to a child who needed extra patience and effort to be heard and seen. Honestly, I didn't know if I had it in me. Not on the day I found out. And I still don't know.

But I'm certain of one thing: she deserves love, and we're going to give it to her. She deserves to be seen and the world will see her. If by her mere existence, she was able to change me as a person, I can't imagine what greater things she may be capable of doing.

During my journey with her, I've interacted with more new people than I can count. Leaving your life in your home country to settle abroad takes a lot, but I've tried my best to form a community.

I look for families with special needs kids and offer them resources I've found through my research. We're on the same path, and at the end of the day, it's overwhelming.

I've focused on staying on top of Bivan's milestones because I missed the bus with Ishanvi. Turns out, he also has delayed speech.

Boys are four times more likely than girls to be diagnosed with autism. That's a statistic. So, I've been cautious of his every move, every word.

It's been an uncertain time. Bivan was born in September 2019, six months before COVID brought the world to an unprecedented pause. We were stuck at home during his first year while I was struggling to deal with Ishanvi's diagnosis, so I didn't give him much attention. By the time we celebrated his first birthday, Ishanvi was making progress thanks to ABA therapy, and my attention shifted.

We were able to enroll him in Early Intervention, a concept I hadn't been aware of when Ishanvi was a baby. I used every resource at my disposal to help him meet his milestones. One year into EI, Pravin and I decided we wanted to rule out the possibility of autism. As usual, there was a long wait. We didn't mind. We weren't in a hurry because we'd begun to see a huge improvement in his speech and motor skills. We were almost positive he was neurotypical. But the combination of genetics and statistics suggested he might be on the spectrum. It was hope against statistics, and I knew better than to rely on hope alone. Not this time.

We put him on the waiting list for testing. Although we'd already gone through the process of finding out if a child was atypical, it was tedious, both mentally and emotionally. As I was filling in the paperwork, memories came back to me. I'd worked very hard to be at peace with Ishanvi's diagnosis, and starting that cycle again made it harder. But this time I had hope. At least, that's what I thought.

In July 2022, we celebrated Ishanvi's birthday at Rocky Mountain National Park. The Monday after we got home, while we were getting back to regular life, I overheard Pravin on his phone. It's not like him to take a call during his busy workday, but I was glad he did. He was talking with the hospital. Someone had cancelled an autism evaluation and we could get in that Wednesday. Pravin looked at me. He said yes. I wished he hadn't.

I thought it might be too early for the evaluation. We could have waited until September, when he was originally scheduled. Once you have a child with autism in the family, the question lingers, "What if a sibling is also autistic?"

It's a tough environment to navigate, but there's no choice.

We were getting tired of the uncertainty, and thought if we found out for sure, we could help him earlier than we'd helped Ishanvi.

Wednesday, July 13, 2022

I didn't like the number thirteen. It didn't feel right.

We had an eight o'clock appointment, and the hospital was an hour's drive from home, so I'd arranged for a sitter to arrive at seven. She'd wait for Ishanvi to wake up, get her ready, and drop her at summer camp.

I was having flashbacks of the day Ishanvi was tested. Bivan had been a baby. Now he was being tested, as well.

We woke up at six and had everything ready. I hadn't told anyone but Pravin's sister who is a doctor. This time, I didn't want to do it alone.

We were at the doctor's office by 7:45, as instructed. A very enthusiastic nurse greeted us with a smile. Bivan didn't like her. She kept touching his hair and telling him how cute he was.

The doctor came in and instructed us to interact with Bivan. We had been through this before, so we followed every instruction without question.

Then a team of therapists moved us to a different room. Bivan seemed to be doing exceptionally well. The occupational therapist kept praising his skills, saying they were on par with his peers. The hope in my heart grew.

After a while, we took a break and grabbed breakfast.

When the testing was completed, the doctor gave us the results. It's amazing how a few hours can dictate the rest of your life.

She said how impressed the team had been with Bivan's skills.

"Come to the point," I thought.

She did. It wasn't what we had expected or hoped for. It was a shock to both of us. Bivan was on the spectrum, as well.

We'd begun the process of testing him as a precautionary measure. We never thought it would become a reality. He was making great progress, but not enough to rule out autism.

The drive back home was unlike any other. Bivan went down for his nap. He must have been tired, getting up early and going through the drill of testing. I was upset and slept on my worries. When we got home, I went to bed, Bivan by my side.

When I woke up, for a moment I didn't remember what had happened and didn't have to know that my son was also autistic, that both my kids were gearing up for a life that could be difficult to navigate.

The first question I had was WHY?

I began to feel anger and frustration. I'd been through this journey before and knew how difficult it was. Having two kids with special needs would be one hell of a task. Just because I had gone through it before didn't mean I was ready to do it again. It felt unfair.

We continued our routine. I took a day off from work to sort out my emotions. Parenting takes so much from you. Sometimes I wonder if I have it in me.

It took me a week to accept Bivan's diagnosis. I'd thought Ishanvi was at the forefront of my struggle. But that summer, almost two years after her diagnosis, Bivan joined the journey. I don't know what the future has in store for us. But I do know that I've figured out a way to accept my kids as they are and help them as much as humanly possible.

I went back to my nine steps from the beginning. I didn't know how powerful my documentation of my journey with Ishanvi would be. In a way, I was preparing for a future I hadn't foreseen, revisiting all my emotions and experiences and trying to do better.

This time, sharing the diagnosis was easier. I still haven't told my side of the family because I'm afraid they'll worry. Pravin told his parents right away. They couldn't believe it. I don't blame them.

The Almighty works in mysterious ways. I can think of a hundred reasons why this is happening to me, but that doesn't help at all.

I know I have to focus on their journey to a healthy, independent life.

Nobody chooses to be the mother of two kids on the spectrum. I figure they came into my life for a reason.

I don't have any regrets about the diagnosis or letting people know that I am raising two special needs kids. I'm trying to erase the stigma, the desire to be seen as "normal."

"As a society, we need to redefine what "normal" is."

No kid should be discriminated against or humiliated because of the way he is. Humanity must step up and help these kids find a footing in this world. I'll do that work as long as I can.

For Ishanvi and Bivan.

For my imperfect family.

Afterword

It's been six months since we went down that unexpected path for the second time. It was hard for Pravin and me, living in a country where family is nonexistent and good friends are hard to come by. But we have each other. The love we found seventeen years ago is still alive, and part of it is running around in the form of two little kids who struggle with so many issues.

We're here for them, every step of the way. We travel, we hike, we help people, we build memories. We live our lives with grace. We're finally building a home filled with memories we've collected over the years.

This is their home, the start of their journey. I cannot guarantee that it will be without bumps. My gut says it won't. But I know those bumps will shape their personalities. I'm not shielding them. I'm preparing them.

I often think of my own journey from a little town in Assam, India to Aurora, Illinois. I've encountered a few bumps myself. But that was my destiny. We are all born with one. I was always destined to be their mother. I hope to be there to see what they are destined for. Until then, I'm filling my heart with love and memories, as many as I can. I have never enjoyed life more than I do now. I'm learning that every moment is precious, and I want to make the most of them.

I've asked all my kids' teachers, therapists and coaches to sign books I'll gift them when they graduate high school.

I make Ishanvi and Bivan write thank you cards to the people who care for them from time to time.

We're teaching them to be grateful and kind.

I now know that in order to realize your potential and enjoy life you must learn gratitude. Not only for the big things, but for all the little things, as well:

Your son's first time on an airplane.

The first concert your daughter performs.

When you realize your parents don't treat your kids differently than they would any other grandchild.

When your brother tells you he loves your daughter like his own and will be there for her no matter what.

When your child's therapist tells you she feels love when she visits your home because she sees positivity and love blossoming there.

I'm grateful for every single blessing.

Our family's struggle is real. We take it one day at a time and embrace it with a smile.

Together, we have created an atmosphere of empathy and understanding, not just in our home but also in our community. Our aim is to build a future in which every kid is treated equally, no matter their needs.

We will continue to do that as long as we live, because that's what we do. We struggle, we evolve, and we build.

For Ishanvi and Bivan.

Being a mother is the hardest job I've ever had. It requires so much time and energy. It demands that I smile, even when I'm deep in sorrow. It demands that I talk to people I never thought I could talk to.

It has made me stronger, in ways I never thought possible. It has made me resilient, in so many ways. It has made me kind to myself and others. It has made me fall in love with my partner all over again because together we are raising two beautiful people who make us proud every day. It has made me appreciate life in a new way. It has made me appreciate the small moments that make up this big, beautiful life.

If someone asks me how I deal with having two kids on the spectrum, I say I don't treat them differently. I just give them a little kindness with a hint of discipline. They're beautiful the way they are. They'll find their paths one day and keep making me proud. But when they need someone to give them a push and hold them tight, I'll be right here. Always.

Someone once said, "Motherhood is the exquisite inconvenience of being another person's everything." I believe that's true.

Parenting has been extremely hard so far, but it's also been worth much more than I ever imagined.

Acknowledgements

Publishing my first book has been tedious but rewarding. At the core of my heart, I want to help as many families as possible by telling them that life has a bigger purpose. Kids with special needs need our love and acceptance more than ever and awareness is the key factor here. What began as a guide for parents whose kids have been recently diagnosed with autism, gradually grew much bigger in substance. The person witnessing this growth with me is Pravin Singh, my husband, my partner. He has been a part of this journey as much as me and this book wouldn't have materialized without his constant encouragement. There are days we are exhausted and we look each other for comfort. We find strength in our love that helps us keep going. I didn't let him read the manuscript till I was comfortable enough and he was always patient with that. It has been an emotionally overwhelming journey for the both of us and we hope that families across the world who are going through the same process are able to find some solace in this book.

My parents Kalpana Mazumdar and Prafulla Mazumdar who for a reason I now know, never stop believing in me. My mother sacrificed everything to raise me and I am forever indebted to her for being a constant source of inspiration.

My friends Manvendra Singh and Indranee Das who have been a part of my writing journey since I started. My lovely friend Deborah Guerra-Sievers who was part of the cover design and concept. She has been a wonderful support throughout this process. My book club A Novel Bunch, for inspiring me to get back to reading and recommending great books for research.

To my editor Joie Davidow, author of five nationally published books and co-founder of L.A. Weekly and L.A. Style magazines, thank you for guiding me throughout the editing process. You have been kind, supportive and I feel blessed to have met you. To Susan, thank you for your editing services.

And, of course, a million thanks to all the readers, booktokers, bookstagrammers, bloggers, journalists, reviewers who supported my cause and the book.

. . . .

MEGHALI MAZUMDAR IS a storyteller and author living in Aurora, Illinois with her husband and two kids.

She is passionate about bringing positive change to the world and aims to remove the stigma associated with special needs kids by bringing more awareness to society. She writes stories of kindness and generosity and often tells them at storytelling events around Chicago.

CONNECT ONLINE

https://talesbytulika.com

meghali_mazumdar_author

Don't miss out!

Visit the website below and you can sign up to receive emails whenever Meghali Mazumdar publishes a new book. There's no charge and no obligation.

https://books2read.com/r/B-A-TXUW-VMPFC

BOOKS2READ

Connecting independent readers to independent writers.